The Role of Student Affairs in Institution-Wide Enrollment Management Strategies

Alan Galsky, Editor

National Association of Student Personnel Administrators, Inc.
Washington, D.C.

The role of student affairs in institution-wide enrollment management strategies / Alan Galsky, editor.—1st. ed.
   p. cm.
Includes bibliographical references.
ISBN 0-931654-14-9
   1. College attendance—United States. 2. College students—United States—Recruiting. 3. Universities and colleges—United States—Admission. 4. Universities and colleges—United States—Administration. I. Galsky, Alan.
   LC148.2.R65 1991
   378.1'05973'068—dc20   91-12320
                                                 CIP

Contents

Contributors

Joel M. Bagby, Senior Vice President, The Barton-Gillet Company, Baltimore, Maryland

Gary R. Bergman, Executive Director, Center for Enrollment Management, Bradley University, Peoria, Illinois

Robert Bertram, Director, Center for Orientation, Testing and Advisement, Bradley University, Peoria, Illinois

Alan Galsky, Associate Provost for Student Affairs, Bradley University, Peoria, Illinois

Nancy Jones, Manager of Publications Division, Noel Levitz Centers for Institutional Effectiveness and Innovations, Inc., Coralville, Iowa

George Keller, Senior Fellow, University of Pennsylvania, Graduate School of Education, Philadelphia, Pennsylvania

Greg Killoran, Executive Director, Center for Cocurricular Development, Bradley University, Peoria, Illinois

Ed King, Executive Director, Center for Housing, Residential Life, and Student Judicial System, Bradley University, Peoria, Illinois

Marlene Kuskie, Professor of Counselor Education, Kearney State University, Kearney, Nebraska

Randi Levitz, Executive Vice President, Noel Levitz Centers for Institutional Effectiveness and Innovations, Inc., Coralville, Iowa

Jane Linnenburger, Executive Director, Center for Career Development, Bradley University, Peoria, Illinois

Lee Noel, President, Noel Levitz Centers for Institutional Effectiveness and Innovations, Inc., Coralville, Iowa

David Pardieck, Associate Director of Enrollment Management and Director of Financial Assistance, Bradley University, Peoria, Illinois

Angela M. Roberson, Associate Director of Enrollment Management for Undergraduate Admissions, Bradley University, Peoria, Illinois

Kathy Thomas, Director of Financial Assistance, DePaul University, Chicago, Illinois

Jim F. Vick, Director, Career Services Center, Eastern Michigan University, Ypsilanti, Michigan

Ray Zarvell, Executive Director, Center for Educational Development, Bradley University, Peoria, Illinois

R. Fred Zuker, Associate Vice Chancellor for Enrollment Management, University of California-Riverside, Riverside, California

Introduction

The Role of Student Affairs in Institution-Wide Enrollment Management Strategies

George Keller

One of the more remarkable changes in America's colleges and universities during the 1980s has been the new duties of campus administrative officers. It is not as profound a change as the extraordinary increase in adult and nontraditional students on the campuses. But the shift to a more active management style to provide stability in enrollments and finances and to facilitate orderly change through strategic planning has been a noticeable one.

Colleges and universities have been described as organizations that are "loosely coupled" (Weick, 1987). That is, most offices and departments are quite independent, often with different goals and with relatively little collaboration or unity in achieving institutional purposes. This situation is still true in most universities and many colleges. But in recent years more institutions have been coupling their operations to avoid decline or painful buffeting from rapidly changing conditions.

Of these new conditions, the changes in the American family and the decline in number of births to below replacement levels for our population are perhaps the most consequential for colleges. The United States is undergoing a one-fourth drop

1

in the number of high school graduates between 1979 and 1995. In addition, fewer secondary school students are taking college preparatory work; so, of the high school graduates left, a diminished number are prepared for college work. For some states this means a decline of one-third or greater in the number of potential students for their colleges.

Universities and colleges have three choices. They can watch their enrollments decrease, lay off faculty and staff, and perhaps eventually go out of business or merge if they are small or financially weak. They can purposefully shrink the size of their student bodies and battle to hold quality, as institutions as varied as Smith College, Franklin and Marshall College, and the University of Tennessee have done. Or they can make themselves more attractive to the really able students and their parents, institute procedures to recruit students more effectively, and provide a more satisfactory four years for the undergraduate experience. A fourth possibility, that of substituting new markets such as adult students to replace lost traditional-age students, has also been widely used.

To those institutions that elect the third option—that of holding size through improved programs of recruiting, financial aid, advising, residence hall life, placement, cafeteria dining, tutoring, and the like—the enrollment management concept has become compelling (Hossler 1986a, 1986b). Through enrollment management, colleges and universities attempt to coordinate several or all of the services that affect students to increase the quality and favorable impact of those services. At the most basic level, the offices of admissions and financial aid are merged. At the most advanced level, all the offices that deal with students, from preparing promotional materials for recruiting and running student activities on campus to the placement office, dormitories, and intramural sports, are brought under a benevolent czar. Dozens of campuses, perhaps as many as 100, currently have new vice presidents of student enrollment who manage a reasonably steady enrollment of quality students despite the demographic downturn.

A few writers have tried to present a taxonomy of the new forms in this embryonic world of enrollment management

(Kemerer, Baldridge & Green, 1982). They believe there may be four. First is a campus committee or task force to which several or many of the offices concerned with student numbers and satisfaction belong. Second is appointment of a part-time or full-time coordinator for all these offices, who diplomatically encourages them to work together more effectively. Third is a matrix approach, which unites various offices concerned with students into several cooperating groups: a recruiting and admissions group, a marketing group, a student academic affairs and retention group, a student social affairs group, etc. A fourth approach is to appoint a full-time vice president responsible for the entire process of managing enrollment stability, from summer programs for 10th and 11th grade students to the graduation ceremony.

The radical underlying commitment of enrollment management is its unswerving focus on the longitudinal care and comprehensive education of students. It is not often admitted but most colleges and universities are run primarily, or at least heavily, for the benefit of the faculty. Enrollment management seeks instead to make students central to enlarge a college's market share of traditional students in a shrinking market. It is a form of one-upmanship in a newly competitive arena. But it is also an effort that benefits the young people who are alleged to be the reason that colleges exist.

Enrollment management requires different ways of doing things. Market research becomes more important because institutions need to keep monitoring what students and significant others think. Parents, who are frequently ignored by colleges and universities, become more important because they are influential in shaping student motivations, choices, and well-being. The quality of student life, of academic advising, and of religious sensibility also become more important. In effect, enrollment management can significantly alter the way a campus, its faculty, and its leaders behave and think about their enterprise.

Few institutions have moved so expertly into enrollment management as Bradley University. Today, Bradley's program is one of the most coherent enrollment management operations in the nation. It is also one of the more successful, with increasing admissions applications to Bradley each year and with a retention rate that brings back nine in ten freshmen for the sophomore year, well above the retention rate for U.S. colleges and universities overall.

Bradley's form of enrollment management is in some ways prototypical and worth serious study by every institution of higher education not flooded by applicants (i.e., perhaps 3,000 of the 3,400 higher education institutions). But it is also unusual. For one reason, Bradley pays remarkable attention to the parents of each student. Two, the chief student affair officer reports to the chief academic officer, not to the president. He is not a vice president of student affairs or a vice president for enrollment but an associate provost. As such he meets with academic deans and department chairs regularly, and is able to bring about changes from the academics on campus, not just from the student services group. Three, the associate provost for student affairs himself is a scholar who has done scientific research, and approaches enrollment stability in a time of decreasing births as an urgent problem in scientific management.

The last of these differences may be a harbinger. In the future, the genial champions of students who make up the majority of student affairs officers may need to yield to a more scholarly, institution-oriented breed: comprehensively shrewd yet caring executives who are as close to deans and professors as they are to students.

Fortunately, this book allows readers at American colleges and universities to peek into the emerging world of enrollment management and to ponder the new demands that face leaders of student affairs. Given the variety of higher education institutions in this country, each reader will view enrollment management with her or his own prism. In these pages one can look at some of the best operational programs in some detail, aided by descriptions from some of the nation's outstanding practitioners of enrollment management.

References

Hossler, D. (ed.) (1986a). *Managing college enrollments.* San Francisco: Jossey-Bass Publisher.

Hossler, D. (1986b). *Creating effective enrollment management systems.* New York: College Entrance Examination Board.

Kemerer, F.; Baldridge, J.V.; and Green, K. (1982). *Strategies for effective enrollment management.* Washington, D.C: American Association of State Colleges and Universities.

Weick, K. (1987). Educational organizations as loosely coupled systems. *Administrative Science Quarterly,* 21, 1–19.

Chapter 1

The Many Roads to Building a Successful Enrollment Management System

Joel M. Bagby

If marketing and marketplace positioning were the buzzwords of the late 1970s and early 1980s in higher education, then surely enrollment management has become the *sine qua non* of the late '80s and early '90s. There are many reasons for this development, not the least of which is the comfortingly scientific ring the words have; like calculus, enrollment management promises to calculate the incalculable, to control the uncontrollable, to render more certain that which often has been intuitive and ad hoc.

Some institutions began to cling to the idea of enrollment management without fully understanding the substance of what it implied and involved. They were not prepared to make the unrelenting commitments to closely coupled management techniques this approach to student population concerns demands. Other institutions, however, have looked at the idea more realistically. Several of these, including some discussed later in this chapter, have successfully embraced its tenets in a coordinated way.

The central text for these converts has been *Strategies for Effective Enrollment Management* (Kemerer, Baldridge & Green,

1982). This excellent volume defines the basic premises for enrollment management, and reflects the discipline needed to integrate all the facets of a student's education, life, and outcomes.

In 1986, the College Board issued the companion document, *Creating Effective Enrollment Management Systems,* by Hossler (1986). In this book, enrollment management is described as the natural evolutionary outcome of at least four major trends in managing the student population function:

- Continual analysis of the institution's image in the student marketplace
- Attention to the connections between recruitment and financial aid policies
- An early willingness to adopt sound marketing principles in recruitment activities (such as exchange of value and consumer satisfaction)
- A recognition of the importance of the gathering and utilization of a continuing flow of information to guide institutional practices and policies.

An earlier volume in the Jossey-Bass New Directions for Higher Education Series, *Marketing Higher Education* (Barton, 1978), dealt with some of these concerns. Clifford C. Campbell, then vice president for enrollment planning at Point Park College in Pittsburgh, wrote in that book

> The chief admissions officer of any college is engaged in an exercise in futility unless he or she copes with the greatest problem in admissions: making the college president and other administrators aware of the importance of their executive role in sensitizing all elements of the college community to the interdependent nature of college admissions as the veritable life blood of the institution.

Thus was being shaped a whole new integrated philosophy of enrollment management, even though it often was not being called by that name.

According to Hossler (1986), pioneers in shaping and implementing these concepts included William Ihlenfeldt, dean of admissions at Northwestern University; Thomas J. Huddleston, Jr., then at Bradley University; and John J. Maguire, then at Boston College. All these professionals in the 1970s sensed the need for fundamental unity of every aspect of a student's education, life, orientation, financial requirements, and placement. They worked to establish at their institutions a systematic approach to the relationships with matriculants that progressed from the initial contact in the student's junior year in high school, until he/she was successfully placed in a job or graduate school (and in some institutions, such as Syracuse University, even beyond that outcome).

Since these early enrollment planners were articulate and nationally visible, their ideas quickly caught on and were polished and extended by many other active enrollment professionals. Soon what had been lecture notes and visual aids for a few workshops and symposia became a way of life for many in the profession. Even more important, those ideas began to receive sympathetic hearing in the president's offices of those institutions which depend mainly on tuition income for their sustenance and good health. And because these strategies usually worked at the institutions that tried them, it was easier to convince other presidents, boards, and financial vice presidents of their value.

In the 1980s, it became clear that there are probably as many ways to develop and implement an enrollment management concept for a college or university as there are institutions willing to take this enlightened approach. This diversity has grown not only out of the varying nature and needs of individual institutions, but also out of the ways their individual marketplaces have changed over time.

And yet, even in the flux of diversity, certain key fundamentals have been retained. These include the following:

1. The student is the center of the enrollment management universe. In all the enrollment management systems which have attracted national attention, the underlying premise has been the focus on the student and his/her academic, personal, and career needs. This idea, of course, was inherent in higher education in America, but commitment to it had been uneven at some institutions. An enrollment management concept restores that focus.

2. The computer is the key to systemization. Almost all the colleges and universities that have developed enrollment management systems implemented, at some phase of their planning, a centralized computer system which tracked applicants, admitted students and matriculants, and which united their financial aid requirements with their application/admission process. These systems took many forms and involved many different kinds of machines, but most of the management approaches taken would not have been possible without them.

3. The chief academic officer serves as catalyst for the process. Academic input and acceptance are critical to a successful enrollment management process. In most cases, the academic vice president or provost has been the engine of change in creating these systems. Also in most cases, it is clear that the provost has been the chief "marketing" officer for the institution—that he/she has been responsible for program design and program delivery—and thus for the marketing position of the institution.

4. Recruitment/retention becomes the central concern of everyone in the college/university, not just of the admissions office. This notable change has taken root slowly but surely. Some faculties have not been receptive to the idea that they are equal partners with the admissions counselors in wooing, winning, and keeping students enrolled, but in the most enlightened (i.e., successful) institutions, faculties have joined in enthusiastically.

5. Recognition of marketing/promotion as the heart of the system is being achieved. Ten years ago, marketing, like the name of Yahweh for early Israelites, could not be spoken aloud on college campuses. Over time, marketing in its most comprehensive sense—the kind of marketing which Philip Kotler refers to as "exchange of value"—has not only come to be accepted but almost swallowed whole. Such phrases as "product lines," "packaging," "segmentation," and "shelf life" now come trippingly off college admissions counselors' lips. And some even have begun to understand the true nature of the

discipline (as witness the emphasis on satisfied consumers). The achievement of the full integration of marketing into student recruitment planning, however, awaits the ability of enrollment management officers to be treated as decision makers in all matters pertaining to program, place, price, and promotion.

6. The importance of ongoing research is being recognized. As the real estate sales people once chanted, "Location, location, and location" for the three most vital words in their profession, now deans of admissions have come to understand that "data, data, and data" are the cornerstones of success in their field. Such important tools of evaluation and measurement as admitted student questionnaires, realistic market surveys, matriculant/nonmatriculant studies, satisfied consumer surveys, and other methods of probing the student market zeitgeist have proven enormously useful in focusing and disciplining enrollment management systems. Another of my colleagues, David Davis Van Atta, former director of institutional research at Oberlin College, has led in establishing the primacy of data and analysis in enrollment management concerns.

7. The effective linkages among strategic planning, institutional differentiation and marketplace success are increasingly being understood. Where once all institutions strove to resemble one or two national models, in the '80s many institutions have come to understand that it was their differences, not their similarities, that would attract more committed applicants. Thus, student-centered strategic planning, too, has become part of workable enrollment management systems.

Admittedly, different institutions have taken hold of these core ideas in different ways and on varying timeframes. But almost all have included them to some degree in their enrollment management systems.

To better understand how these fundamentals were customized by individual institutions, we now will look at three leading examples of how an enrollment management concept has been developed, installed, and improved in recent years.

The institutions represented here differ in geography, complexity, and size. One is a comprehensive research university of 15,000 students in southeastern United States; a second is a comprehensive university in the lower Midwest enrolling about 6,000 students; the third is a small liberal arts women's college with a largely commuter population. What all three have in common has been a quick recognition of an approaching enrollment crisis or new requirement and a visionary enrollment management response. Their differentiation has more to do with the form of those responses and the application they made of the precepts of enrollment management than with their institutional profile.

Example 1
Bradley University: Up the Down Demographics

Bradley University had a history of being concerned for its students' welfare and outcomes long before the 1970s. From its founding by Lydia Moss Bradley in 1897, Bradley has been an institution which specialized in undergraduate education and close personal attention for its students. But an enrollment crisis in 1977 forced the university to review all the ways it dealt with prospective as well as enrolled students, in terms of winning them and retaining them once they matriculated. The declining demographics of Illinois (source of 75 percent of Bradley's students) and the Great Lakes region made this an urgent consideration.

To gain true perspective on how well students' educations were being tailored to their needs, the university instituted at that time a new concept of student and prospective student relationships. Soon this concept embraced improved planning and performance in admissions, financial aid, orientation, academic advising, retention, and the center for career development. As these departments became more unified, more effective, and more visible to their "customers," Bradley's graduates, they soon began to have the desired effect of increased attractiveness for new students and of decreasing attrition among enrolled students.

By the end of the 1970s, Bradley had centralized all aspects of student life outside the classroom into an office of student affairs, administered by an associate provost of the university. This officer, working directly with the chief academic officer, was able to provide the optimum working environment for recruiting and retaining students.

These steps were further fortified when Bradley instituted an Academic Exploration Program, which allowed undecided students to fulfill basic general education requirements without losing time toward degrees in their chosen fields. This plan also allowed them to qualify for their chosen major—even if it were one of the more competitive fields at Bradley.

Other effective recruitment and retention steps in the 1980s included full computerization of the Bradley campus (two residence halls of the future featured personal computers in every room and telecommunications capacity across the entire campus); strengthening of orientation and placement programs; and intensified guidance and academic counseling by hand-picked faculty members. In addition, the university completed a strategic plan in the early 1980s which included a revitalization of the core curriculum and a reinforcing of Bradley's basic programmatic strengths and distinction.

Throughout all these discussions, the university's financial aid planners played a major role. More than four-fifths of all Bradley's undergraduates receive aid in some form. Thus the flexibility and innovativeness of financial support have won many candidates to the university simply because of Bradley's willingness to tailor aid to the needs of the individual.

One other feature of Bradley's enrollment management system deserved attention. In the early 1980s, the university closely studied the students currently enrolled at Bradley in terms of ability levels, financial background, and zip code origins. The university conducted an analysis of accessible regions of the country with pockets of students showing similar profiles. As a result of this new market study, the university placed regional representatives in such key existing and prospective markets as St. Louis, Chicago, Minneapolis, the Ohio Valley, and the New York metropolitan region to help maintain strengthened contact with prospects in more distant markets. Each of these areas since has been productive in developing new applicants and students.

In 1987, recognizing that the university was now in an entirely new competitive set, Bradley completely revitalized and redirected its recruitment communications and moved to a position of greater selectivity and national visibility.

Most at Bradley credit the university's success to the determination of the Bradley administration to serve students' needs first, and to the growing awareness among student affairs professionals that only by creating such a student-centered environment could the university remain fully competitive in its student recruitment marketplace.

Table 1 represents Bradley's productivity in applications, matriculants, and retention in the past five years, all achieved in the face of declining demographics in the university's primary and secondary markets.

Table 1
Summary of Bradley University's Freshman Applications,
Enrollment and Retention
1984–1989

	1985	1986	1987	1988	1989
Applications	2297	2268	2777	3214	3475
Freshman Enrollment	707	825	965	1011	1110
% Retention Freshman-Sophomore Year	90.4	89.7	86	NA	NA
% Annual Retention Rate	87.6	89.3	98.0	89.8	NA

Example 2
University of Miami: The Power of Effective Leadership

In the mid-1970s, admissions officers at the University of Miami realized that to recruit the group of 3,000 new students the university required each year to meet its economic model, the university had to win one out of every 36 students who made a private college choice. Obviously, this was a daunting assignment at a time in which the university's tuition costs were rising rapidly and the cost of sustaining contact with Miami's largely national market was rising.

There were other characteristics of the university's student-population profile that were equally unsettling: a 60–40 mix of national students to Florida students, a large pool of high-risk students who needed some remedial help, high freshman-year attrition rates, and some indication that many enrolled students were giving their education low ranking on their priority list of things to worry about.

In addition, one survey of alumni revealed a high proportion (more than half) who would not choose the university if they had that decision to make again.

In 1981 an energetic new president, Edward T. Foote II, former dean of the law school at Washington University at St. Louis, was named at the university. He quickly instituted an era of rapid change. He set out to redefine the Miami mission and its identity, to redesign public parts of its campus, to strengthen its faculty and overall academic climate, and to begin the process of rekindling pride in its alumni and friends. In addition, he determined that the university would begin re-invigorating the University of Miami's Florida base and would become less dependent on recruitment in faraway places.

Although not everyone was aware of it at the time, the process the university established to begin dealing with this new mandate was in reality an enrollment management system. Specific steps included:

- A merger of the office of admissions and the office of financial aid, which allowed students to know what their aid package was as soon as they were admitted.
- Creation of a new Florida strategy which would place great emphasis on bringing the good news of the university's new positioning to the major urban areas of the state and begin to attract the best Florida students to the University of Miami. Once valedictorians from Florida

high schools began choosing Miami, the next tier of students was sure to follow.

- Development of a new management system for both admissions and financial aid administered by an associate provost for undergraduate studies and directed by two experienced professionals who knew and understood both Florida and national markets.
- An overhaul of the university's honors program. This included an expansion of the number of students admitted to this program, an increase in the number of honors scholarships granted, and creation of an honors residence hall with personal computers and telecommunications capacity.
- An intensified program of marketing research and planning, including surveys of matriculants and non-matriculants, as well as an in-depth survey of attriting students.
- Development of a new strategic plan for the university which took into consideration its unique location; its distinctive programs in marine biology, law, and medicine; and its strong connections with the economic development interests of the south Florida region. This plan resulted in a university that was smaller but better, or "leaner and meaner" in the campus vernacular of the time.
- A revitalized public affairs program which included all new university recruitment publications, new identity and special segmented documents for honors students and such special interest audiences as business administration and science students.

In addition, two unforeseen environmental forces boosted the university's efforts: the South Florida economic climate boomed and the university's football team, guided by a succession of strong-armed quarterbacks and driven by formidable defenses, began to win national championships and to appear frequently on national television.

This combination of good management and good fortune resulted in dramatic upsurge in all the university's recruitment numbers, and, almost simultaneously, a drop-off in the attrition rate. Today, the University of Miami is a notable national success story in its recruitment and retention interests. And those staff members who participated in the process are quick to credit the vision and aggressive leadership of President Foote, as well as the enthusiastic support of the Board of Trustees and the entire university community. A recent highly successful capital campaign has raised almost half a billion dollars, thus ensuring even more promising outcomes for this global university.

Table 2 reveals the university's increase in applicants and matriculants in 1986–88.

Table 2
Summary of Miami University's Applications
and Enrollments
1986–1988

	New Freshmen		
	1986	**1987**	**1988**
Applications	5662	5425	8241
Admissions	4360	4317	5069
Enrollment	1692	1734	1900

Example 3
Alverno College: Applying Enrollment
Management Concepts to the Adult Learner

Each Friday afternoon during the school year at Alverno College near Milwaukee, Marlene Neises, director of Alverno's academic services, makes a white glove inspection of all the teaching and learning facilities to be used during the next 2-1/2 days by weekend college students (and that includes all the facilities available on the Alverno campus—from classrooms to the library to the computer labs to the rest rooms). If she finds anything amiss—even a shortage of toilet paper—it is fixed, and fixed quickly.

This attention to detail tells much about Alverno and its approach to enrollment management for its weekend college students. No compromises are allowable when it comes to the interests and welfare of these educational consumers. Nor is compromise possible in another program Alverno has developed for all its students, both weekday and weekend, called ability-based education. Alverno has deservedly gained national attention for its focus on the educational needs of all its students and the ways it measures the ability of its graduates to meet the demands of the workday world.

Both emphases at Alverno have grown out of a well-conceived, well-planned enrollment management approach in which nothing that pertains to students' education is out of court for the educators and managers at Alverno. In that spirit, the only verbal differentiation Alverno makes between its types of students is the time they choose to be educated, weekday or weekend.

How Alverno came to develop these emphases has to do with the history and tradition of the college and with its commitment to meeting the expectations of its students as well as its alumnae, friends and supporters, and regional employers.

First, a word about the college itself: Founded in 1887 by the School Sisters of Saint Francis, Alverno is a small liberal arts college for women with about 2,300 students enrolled on a headcount basis and about 1,700 students as full-time equivalents. Its programs feature the arts and sciences, management, education, and nursing. Enrollment at the 50-acre suburban campus is about 90 percent from Wisconsin, and largely commuter.

As at many other institutions, enrollment management concepts came to Alverno in bits and pieces. "It was evolutionary, not revolutionary, in our case," a college spokesman explained. The first step was the college's determination to attend to the needs of the woman adult learner. Many discussions of the late 1960s and '70s were focused on the pool of able and interested women students in the Milwaukee region who had not completed their degrees but appeared to be willing and eager to do so. Alverno, with its suburban location and reality-based program offerings, seemed ideally positioned to offer a real educational service to these students.

The second key decision was not to sequester the adult learner services or education from the more traditional mission of the college. Although it was clear from the outset that weekends were the most convenient time for many of the degree-completion students to attend Alverno, it was also clear that the program would not work if they were given second-class citizen status in any way. Thus, all the offices on campus which delivered student services to weekday students also were opened on weekends to deliver those same services. Advising, counseling, financial aid, registrar, and all other student functions were as accessible to weekend students as to weekday.

And, more to the point, all the learning support systems required by students in the weekend college would be open at those traditionally closed hours. Faculty and staff made the scheduling adjustments over time with good will, reports indicate, but "Mondays around here can be awfully dead after a weekend college session," one Alverno staffer pointed out.

When Alverno first planned its weekend college format in 1977 (modeled to some extent after that of Mundelein College outside Chicago, which had opened in 1974), administrators had anticipated about 50 students for the first term. Instead, 251 women registered and attended, and the enrollments have not slowed down since that time. Enthusiasm engendered enthusiasm, and word of mouth among degree-completion students has been Alverno's strongest asset. Currently, weekend college enrollments total 1,136, and the total has been growing steadily.

Enrollment management was a phrase waiting to be coined when Alverno began a far-reaching overhaul of its curriculum in the early '70s. But the distinctive curriculum that resulted—a highly individualized approach that helps students apply knowledge, not just remember it—became a working academic platform for the enrollment management practices that evolved at the college in the '80s.

Alverno's ability-based curriculum has twin goals: acquiring the knowledge traditionally associated with a liberal arts degree plus developing the abilities needed to apply it. The abilities, which must be demonstrably mastered by graduation, are:

- Communication
- Analysis
- Problem solving
- Values in decision making
- Social interaction
- Taking responsibility for the environment
- Involvement in the contemporary world
- Aesthetic response.

A new method of judging student progress emerged along-side the emphasis on abilities. Instead of traditional tests, Alverno students take "assessments" that help judge how well students can apply knowledge in a variety of situations.

Alverno uses measurements such as videotape and outside assessments from Milwaukee businesses employing Alverno graduates to test the graduates' abilities. Students in each of Alverno's academic and professional programs also engage in sponsored, off-campus learning activities in which they must apply their abilities in concrete situations.

Best measurement of their effectiveness can be seen in the college's placement figures. Over 90 percent of Alverno's graduates acquire jobs related to their major within six months of graduation. In addition, 88 percent of Alverno's freshmen return each year as sophomores, and fully 70 percent of all students, weekend and weekday, who begin at Alverno ultimately receive their degrees. For students who have attended Alverno, the integration of academic, pragmatic, and career interests, along with a thoroughly focused effort to give fullest attention to the needs of both weekday and weekend students, have made this educational experience well worth the investment and effort. According to surveys of Milwaukee and regional businesses, the Alverno product is perceived to be distinctive and productive.

The growth of enrollment at Alverno's weekend college from 1980–89 is shown in Figure 1.

Figure 1
ALVERNO ENROLLMENT GROWTH

	Weekend	Weekday

Weekday values (middle labels): 704, 796, 807, 847, 894, 895, 1028, 1085, 1106, 1136

Weekend values (bottom labels): 659, 576, 552, 591, 617, 809, 804, 897, 1085, 1174

Years: 1980-81, 1981-82, 1982-83, 1983-84, 1984-85, 1985-86, 1986-87, 1987-88, 1988-89, 1989-90

YEAR

Summary

It can be seen from these examples that a certain chemistry needs to exist at tuition-driven institutions for an enrollment management concept to become feasible:

- Uncertainty about the stability of existing student markets, that is the status quo probably cannot be maintained
- Visionary leadership which understands that recruitment and retention are total institutional responsibilities
- A willingness to change the ways the admissions/recruitment function has historically been managed
- A faculty receptive to playing a more active role in confronting student population concerns
- Sufficient programmatic appeal to undergird new approaches to enrollment management
- Realistic markets for the institution's services which can be molded to greater degrees of receptivity
- Professional staff willing to redouble efforts once an institutional positioning concept has been developed.

Given these underlying factors, and an institutional willingness to invest in change, the development and implementation of varying strategies for enrollment management can be assured some chances of success.

References

Barton, D.W. (ed.) (1978). *New directions for higher education:
Marketing higher education.* San Francisco: Jossey-Bass
Publisher.

Hossler, D. (1986). *Creating effective enrollment management
systems.* New York: The College Board.

Kemerer, F.; Baldridge, J.V.; and Green, K. (1982). *Strategies
for effective enrollment management.* Washington, D.C.:
American Association of State Colleges and Universities.

Chapter 2

Enrollment Management in the Private University

Gary R. Bergman

As colleges and universities across the country enter the last decade of this century, increased attention will be focused on enrollment management models to identify, monitor, and control student enrollment patterns. For many private institutions, the ability to attract and retain sufficient quantities of quality students has become a primary strategic planning objective. With institutional survival so dependent on stable enrollments, resources must be allocated for identifying, recruiting, admitting, enrolling, and retaining qualified candidates who meet the institutional student profile.

For the past decade, collegiate administrators have had extensive documentation projecting decreases in the pool of 18- to 22-year-olds through the early 1990s (Hutchinson, 1978). Demographers, forecasters, statisticians, and educational consultants indicate that these declines will signal fiscal hardship for many institutions across the country. With declining birth rates, escalating tuition costs, and reduced levels of financial assistance, private institutions have, in record numbers, been forced to reexamine their strategic enrollment and retention objectives.

With many private institutions dependent upon stable enrollments for fiscal survival, the need for stronger recruitment and retention programs is clear. As these institutions examine their market position and plan enrollment strategies, they are becoming increasingly aware of proven marketing procedures designed to analyze, plan, and implement more effective recruitment programs. For many institutions, this is a long and difficult progress due to limited funds, inexperienced marketing personnel, lack of historical admissions and financial assistance data, and, for many schools, a real commitment to make the enrollment management process an institutional priority.

As institutions look to marketing concepts to address enrollment concerns, they are often tempted to focus attention exclusively on programs within their own admissions and financial assistance areas. Here, resources are usually provided to enhance traditional recruitment programs such as increasing travel budgets, upgrading promotional literature, expanding direct mail and telemarketing functions, and initiating new financial assistance and scholarship packaging programs. Unfortunately, many of these activities do not produce the desired long-term results necessary to stabilize or increase enrollment objectives (Topor, 1983).

In the past several years, many private institutions have made significant progress in establishing effective recruitment and retention programs by designing comprehensive enrollment management models. Increasingly, institutions realize that comprehensive admissions recruitment and marketing programs must reflect the total environment encountered by students; and not simply mirror activities promoted by the admissions office. In past years (and even at an alarming number of institutions today), the marketing and the management of enrollments have been limited to contacts between prospective students, parents, admissions personnel, and selective members of the faculty.

Today, however, effective enrollment management recruitment programs fully integrate traditional admissions programs with those involving all areas of student services. Recruitment programs that directly provide students with exposure to academic, career development and placement programs, cocurricular activities, and residential life will have a significant positive impact on a student's college selection decision (Peat, Marwick, & Main, 1977).

Conducting recruiting programs exclusively within the offices of admissions and financial assistance has obvious limitations. While traditional admissions office services provide an adequate "initial" exchange of information to prospective students, they often fail to address long-term student needs relating to academic, social, recreational, cultural, and professional opportunities. Admissions and enrollment management recruitment programs that do not reflect the full range of student interests and needs within student services are short-sighted. Often, they provide only short-term solutions and do not resolve long-term enrollment stability concerns (Kotler & Fox, 1985).

An Effective Model

The development of an effective enrollment management model should reflect the institution's total image, its mission, the scope of its academic programs, and the real life, day-to-day environment in which students live and interact. The model must reflect the opportunities, programs, and conditions in which students function as a member of the institution's community (Hossler, 1984). Information on living conditions, residential life, retention rates, placement opportunities, student perceptions and attitudes all need to be identified and analyzed before the model can be effectively implemented. The enrollment management model will pay particular attention to these factors as they relate to the following areas.

Academic Quality
As the overall pool of collegiate candidates continues to decline, the pool of high quality students will find themselves in a highly marketable situation (Graff, 1985). For high-ability students, opportunities for scholarship and grant programs, special academic course offerings, and campus visits will increase by institutions across the country.

With large investments being made to attract new students,

the enrollment management model must reflect the institution's profile for academic quality. The model must take into consideration the current composition of its students and the direction in which the institution desires to proceed over the next decade. For many private institutions, maintaining or increasing academic quality of the new class, while stabilizing enrollment headcount, will be an increasingly difficult objective.

Recruitment Programs

Programs, activities, and procedures available within the student affairs area will need to be analyzed and reviewed on a consistent basis if they are to be an effective aspect of the enrollment management model.

Some examples of campus and off-campus recruitment programs which can effectively involve student affairs include:

- Programs involving high school students and members of the Career Development Center. Here, students can learn firsthand of opportunities relating to interviewing skills, securing employment, acceptance to graduate or professional school.
- Opportunities for students to work with the Center of Educational Development to identify and consider academic areas relating to their skills and interests and programs to enhance time management and study skills.
- Programs to enhance the understanding of financial planning and budgetary opportunities for parents to meet the escalating cost of higher education.

Recruitment activities must be coordinated to work in conjunction with programs conducted by the functional student affairs areas of counseling, testing, career development, cocurricular activities, admissions, financial assistance, and residential life. In this role, the enrollment management model must actively provide programs and opportunities for all areas affecting student life to share and exchange information within the model.

Enrollment Projections

A key element of the enrollment management model is the ability to study enrollment trends and identify areas for the institution to monitor and record student interests. By establishing methods to identify trends, track yields of prospects and applicants, and monitor levels of academic progress, the enrollment management model will enhance the quality and accuracy of its enrollment projections.

One of the major benefits of a successful enrollment management model is its ability to identify trends as they occur rather than after they have taken place. For many institutions, the ability to track the current prospect and applicant pool and analyze its demographic distribution, academic area of interest, application date, initial source of contact, and students' financial resources can provide invaluable predictive information on the size and quality of the incoming class.

Center for Enrollment Management

With substantial changes in demographics, financial assistance packaging, admissions budgets, inflation, and recruitment strategies, it is increasingly important that institutions review their strategic mission to examine their position in the educational marketplace. Here, the Center for Enrollment Management can rely on established business marketing concepts to determine the institution's identity from both an internal and external perspective. How the marketplace views the institution should prove to be as important as how the institution views itself.

For many colleges and universities, utilizing business marketing concepts is an uncomfortable, time consuming, and difficult process. While many private institutions have utilized marketing concepts, many have only recently begun to utilize research to identify and analyze their strengths, weaknesses, and opportunities for improvement. An effective marketing research program will enable the institution to evaluate the various "perception levels" which exist in the marketplace. Understanding the perception levels of prospective and enrolled students, parents, faculty, administration, counselors, and alumni are essential in determining market awareness.

In developing a marketing awareness program, the Center for Enrollment Management must carefully evaluate the institution's identity and the message that is sent (and is being received) to prospective students and their parents. An integral part of this process is a consistent and systematic review of all programs which are being communicated to the public. This process will include a review of the following outreach programs:

- Admissions and financial assistance publications, newsletters, flyers, catalogs, student search mailings, electronic mail services
- Media materials, including press releases, newspaper and magazine advertisements, television and radio spots
- Promotional materials, including VHS tapes, video discs, films, cassettes, slide shows, pc diskettes
- Alumni and development publications, newsletters, flyers, fund-raising literature
- Materials distributed by members of the faculty, administration, and all areas within student services.
- Student publications, newsletters, campus radio and television stations, campus posters

Critical to a review of these outreach programs is the impression created by their use. The Center for Enrollment Management, through the use of survey, inventory analysis, and comprehensive market analysis, must be able to provide answers to the following questions: How are these outreach materials perceived? How do students and parents identify with the institution as a result of their use? Is there a single message being sent or . . . is there confusion being created by mixed messages? Is the desired institution image clearly being promoted?

An effective enrollment management marketing plan attempts to coordinate these areas of promotion to ensure that a clear message is being conveyed to enhance the institution's image. A confusing or misleading image will unquestionably hinder recruiting programs and all opportunities for enrollment sta-bility.

In developing a market awareness program, significant information must be exchanged within all areas of the institution's division of student services: admissions, financial assistance, orientation, retention, cocurricular activities, educational development, and residential life areas. These areas provide invaluable information on student needs, interests, preferences, and their level of satisfaction within the institution. With a clear understanding of students' perceptions, an evaluation of the institution's position in the marketplace is made much easier.

The opportunity for the Center for Enrollment Management to secure market information from resources within student affairs is unlimited. By sharing information between offices within student services on a consistent and regular basis, the Center for Enrollment Management will have an excellent opportunity to control the direction it will need to take.

An institutional management plan developed by the Center for Enrollment Management is affected by available market research information, its budget, the experience level of professionals and support staff, the institution's organizational structure, and the level of involvement and cooperation by members of the university faculty and administration. The development and advancement of an enrollment plan will prove to be a challenge for the center as it assesses resources in terms of their limitations and availability.

To be effective in developing the management plan, the Center for Enrollment Management will need to involve selected areas of the academic community as well as all areas within student services. The center will need the understanding and support of the institution's leadership, including the president, vice presidents, provosts, deans, directors, and department chairs. With an institutional commitment to enrollment management, a plan can be designed, reviewed, and implemented with the knowledge it will be supported at the institution's highest level. Further, the center will need to review the institution's strategic goals (in terms of enrollment objectives) to construct a marketing plan that will achieve the desired enrollment objectives.

In working with the academic community, an effective level

of cooperation and trust is required to enable faculty to understand the institution's enrollment management plan and become a contributing and integral part of its implementation. For many institutions, this is a difficult task due to the minimal level of interaction between faculty and administration. And, with little awareness of the extent of marketing programs being conducted by enrollment management offices, faculty often have limited appreciation of the amount of time, work, and effort being conducted to achieve institutional enrollment objectives.

An effective way to enhance communication with faculty is the development of "faculty liaison" programs. With the support of the leading academic official (provost, vice presidents, academic affairs, etc.), a core group of interested and concerned faculty can be designated as admissions liaisons to meet with members of the Center for Enrollment Management. Here, issues ranging from enrollment trends, demographic changes, market share yield rates to publication development, staff selection, application review, student interviews to academic concerns relating changes in academic major preferences, faculty work loads, achievement and placement tests can be discussed in an open, constructive, and positive environment.

By meeting with faculty liaisons on a regular basis, the Center for Enrollment Management can make significant progress to involve faculty in the institutional enrollment management plan. Here, enrollment data can be reviewed to provide the liaisons with up-to-date information on recruitment, admissions and financial assistance programs. Experience has shown that within a relatively short period of time, faculty become interested and more involved with enrollment management issues and often provide invaluable support to advance the institutional plan. And as liaisons formally report back to their academic areas, additional faculty become involved in what is being accomplished within the enrollment management program. Over time, liaison programs are highly effec-tive in creating strong bonds between enrollment management and the institution's faculty.

While the benefits of involving the leadership of student services will be discussed later in this chapter, it is necessary to emphasize the importance of their commitment and involvement to the Center for Enrollment Management. To effectively construct an institutional plan, it is essential that the Center for Enrollment Management meet frequently (weekly if possible) with the administrative leadership of admissions, financial assistance, career development, residential life, cocurricular activities, retention, and orientation. Such interaction will have substantial positive benefits while allowing each area to contribute to and benefit from opportunities relating to enrollment management. Meetings should address issues relating to enrollment trends, recruitment programs, retention issues, and their interaction with campus life, housing opportunities, health services, placement opportunities, the student cultural and recreational environment, and all other areas relating to student services.

Planning and preparing for change is a concept which has strong implications for activities responsible to the Center for Enrollment Management. With the previously discussed changes in demographics, increased tuition and living costs, declining birth rates, and college preference options, institutions must understand their position in the marketplace and be able to react to changes as they occur, not after they occur.

Sensitivity to changes in the marketplace creates a high "awareness level" which many colleges and universities should strive for if they are to achieve enrollment stability. More than ever, institutions must monitor and review their institutional plan and image in both the general education market and against their leading competitors. This level of self-examination is fast becoming an integral aspect of the enrollment management model due to the pace at which institutional images and perceptions can change.

There are many areas in which the institution must be sensitive to change in the marketplace, including:

1. Institutions must be acutely aware of their position in the education marketplace to determine when changes occur.

Some areas to monitor include:

- The traditional student population versus the nontraditional student mix
- The ratio of part-time students to full-time students
- The percentage of day students to evening students
- The commuter population versus resident population
- The percentages of the class requiring financial assistance, institutional gift aid, and average package

2. One of the most important areas to monitor within the enrollment management model is the prospective and applicant pools. With many institutions critically dependent upon the size of the entering new class, considerable attention is required to analyze the pool of students who are currently interested in the institution. Several areas worthy of attention include:

- Extent of cross-applications by academic area of interest with competing institutions
- Ratio and changes of in-state versus out-of-state students
- Academic quality of the students inquiring and applying for admission
- Changes in demographic distribution of inquiring and applying students
- Ratio of campus visitors versus noncampus visitors

3. As student interest and academic preference change each year, it is important that the Center for Enrollment Management pay particular attention to the academic area of interest of prospective students. Several areas for review include:

- What academic programs are receiving strong attention? Why has interest increased?
- What academic programs are receiving less attention? Are there reasons why interest should not be higher?
- Are there issues relating to yields for specific academic areas?
- Are there local or national trends affecting academic preference?

With increasing cost to finance the collegiate experience, private institutions must be especially sensitive to the relationships between published cost, financial assistance opportunities, and actual adjusted costs. The Center for Enrollment Management must be sensitive to this market to ensure that their financial assistance outreach program is being effectively communicated to the marketplace. Additional detailed information on the important role played by financial assistance is documented in Chapter Three.

In summary, institutions need to be especially concerned to implement an enrollment management model which places significant attention on market sensitivity. Procedures that will monitor and detect changes early in the prospect/applicant cycle and positively respond to them will have good opportunities to achieve their enrollment objectives.

In its most effective role, the Center for Enrollment Management has a special opportunity to identify and promote special academic and student life programs which exist at the institution. When programs of significant interest are identified, considerable time and resources should be employed to develop a specialized recruitment strategy to maximize their enrollment potential to the marketplace.

For many institutions, these opportunities extend beyond traditional academic areas and are often found in support areas reporting to offices within the student services division. When identified, the Center for Enrollment Management should review each program to determine its potential for targeted promotion, which, it is hoped, will position the institution separate and apart from its competitors.

As part of the enrollment management strategy, several areas providing opportunities for special enrollment programs include:

Are there highly specialized academic areas or accredited programs available that can be only found at a few institutions? What are these programs and why are they so special? Is there a market for these programs? And if so, is that market large enough to justify a targeted market promotional plan?

Does the institution maintain laboratories or classrooms with specialized teaching or research equipment? Is this equipment available at other institutions? Why is it special? Is there an opportunity to market these facilities in a way that will be different from competing institutions?

Faculty members who have received significant recognition for teaching and/or research are a valuable resource to the institution. The ability to identify key faculty members for the achievement and to promote their involvement can be an important and significant competitive advantage.

What are the facilities and support services worth promoting to students within residential life? career development? counseling and testing? cocurricular activities? At many institutions, student-centered programs are very beneficial and worthy of promotion. Programs which reflect these student services areas are often of high interest to prospective students and their parents and should be promoted when possible.

As evidenced throughout this chapter, the Center for Enrollment Management has an unlimited opportunity to enhance institutional enrollment by involving areas within student services and the university community. With a strong commitment and leadership, the Center for Enrollment Management can be highly effective in providing strong leadership for the programs relating to all areas within student services.

To involve areas of the university, the Center for Enrollment Management must position itself to identify priority areas of opportunity within the institution which are essential for growth and development.

With significant numbers of alumni and parents (of enrolled) students already involved and knowledgeable of the institution, programs can be developed to enhance promotional and recruiting opportunities in the enrollment management model. For many institutions, one-to-one contact involving alumni and parents with prospective students and their parents can be invaluable in supporting the recruitment effort. Many institutions find that parents and alumni are a willing and ready resource just waiting for direction from the institution to coordinate their involvement.

As a group, faculty, staff, and administration often prove to be a valuable resource in assisting the institution to affect enrollment opportunities. In this area, faculty can assist the Center for Enrollment Management by representing the enrollment effort in college day and night programs, interviewing prospective students, hosting reception programs, sponsoring telemarketing programs, writing letters and cards to interested students, sponsoring phone-a-thons, and developing open-house programs.

Probably one of the most underutilized resources to affect enrollment programs is the use of the enrolled student body. As the most informed and satisfied market available to enrollment management managers, the current student body often provides a unique and highly qualified target group to help affect enrollment programs.

Enrolled students can often be utilized to establish a comprehensive telemarketing program to contact prospective students during the summer and fall months and admitted students during critical winter and spring months. By establishing paid or volunteer telemarketing student groups, significant information can be obtained to determine institution image, the effectiveness of the institution's projected image, and the direction of the enrollment management plan. In utilizing a student-to-student approach, significant information can be obtained to enhance (or alter) the direction of the enrollment management plan.

While these areas are certainly worthy of consideration by centers for enrollment management, it is clear that interaction with student service areas will continue to play a significant role. Interaction with all areas of student services and enrollment management centers is not only important but essential to institutional growth and stability.

References

Graff, A. (1985). Enrollment management: Today and tomorrow, Remarks Presented at The College Board, Chicago, Illinois.

Hossler, D. (1984). *Enrollment management: An integrated approach.* New York: The College Board.

Hutchinson, G. (1978). Importance of recruitment in the 1990's *Journal of the American Association of Collegiate Registrars and Admissions Officers,* 63, 2.

Kotler, P., and Fox, F.A. (1985). *Marketing strategies for educational institutions.* Englewood Cliffs, New Jersey: Prentice-Hall.

Peat, Marwick & Main (1977). Enrollment management in higher education, Executive summary of a survey conducted by Peat Marwick. New York: Peat Marwick Main & Co.

Topor, R. (1983). *Marketing higher education: A practical guide.* New York: Council for Advancement and Support of Education.

Chapter 3

Enrollment Management in the Public University

R. Fred Zuker

Enrollment management is an organizational concept which has gained acceptance at major public universities over the past five to ten years (Hossler, 1984; Ihlenfeldt, 1980; Ingersoll, 1988). Private colleges and universities came earlier to the conclusion that it was necessary to better manage the recruitment and retention functions of the institution. To successfully achieve enrollment goals required more comprehensive management than provided by the often disparate offices of student recruitment and student affairs.

Regardless of institutional type the basic definition of enrollment management remains the same:

> A process or an activity that influences the size, the shape, and the characteristics of a student body by directing institutional efforts in marketing, recruitment and admission as well as pricing and financial aid. In addition, the process exerts a significant influence on academic advising, institutional research agenda, orientation, retention studies, and student services. It is not simply an administrative process. Enrollment management involves the entire campus (Hossler, 1984).

Comprehensive Campus Cooperation:
The Heart of Enrollment Management

The criterion which most completely characterizes the success of enrollment management on any campus, particularly the public institution, is the degree to which the entire campus is involved in recruitment and retention. The enrollment manager must be able to marshall the forces of the entire campus if enrollment goals are to be achieved.

The structure of enrollment management organizations vary widely. The following is an example of an enrollment management organization:

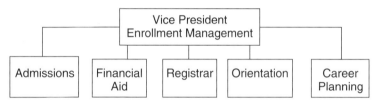

These units may be grouped differently from campus to campus. The general philosophy of enrollment management is to consolidate those offices which have the greatest influence on recruitment and retention under one management leader who has direct access to the most senior level of administration on the campus. Without this direct link to the top there will not be an effective voice for enrollment planning and policy making at the executive level. There will not be a comprehensive view of what needs to be done to enhance recruitment and retention activities and the importance of the enrollment management function will be lost in the welter of competing campus units.

The associate vice chancellor for enrollment management at the University of California at Riverside reports directly to the executive vice chancellor, the chief academic officer for the campus. The vice chancellor for student affairs also reports to the executive vice chancellor. This reporting allows for cooperation between enrollment management and student affairs offices. The units within enrollment management also work closely with the units supervised by the vice chancellor for university relations and development. Maintaining close working relationships with these offices is crucial to the success of enrollment management.

Operational Definitions of Enrollment Management Offices and Officers

Vice President, Enrollment Management. Creating a division of enrollment management requires the consolidation of units which have historically reported to different managers. This means that someone will be losing a portion of a portfolio. As enrollment management divisions are created in the public universities this may present some problems in organizational structures which tend to be rigid and of long standing. The vice president for enrollment management or the chief enrollment management officer will be required to face that challenge from the first day. Once the concept of enrollment management has gained wide acceptance and has matured as a management entity, this factor will disappear; but this will not happen until the current generation of administrators have completed their careers.

Today's enrollment managers will find some skepticism in the work place particularly at the public university where there may be a perception that there is no need for such dramatic organizational overhaul. Existing enrollment and retention conditions may mitigate this situation if it is clear there is a need to create such an organization to deal with an imminent enrollment crisis. One of the first jobs of the new vice president for enrollment management will be to educate the campus about the configuration and function of enrollment management. This task will be made much easier if the impetus is given by the chief executive officer.

An example of such support would be a luncheon hosted by the chief executive officer to which campus, community, and local school leaders are invited. This would give the chief executive officer an opportunity to introduce the concept of enrollment management as well as the new person who has assumed the responsibility.

The chief enrollment management officer will need to quickly establish a strong working relationship with faculty and staff across the campus. He or she will need to assess the current state of recruitment and retention on campus and begin implementing programs to deal with immediate problems. The type of person needed to fill this role will be a combination of strong attributes. What follows is a list of desirable achievements and qualities for such a person:

- Earned doctorate; some teaching experience is highly desirable
- History of progressive responsibility in offices which deal directly with recruitment and/or retention.
- Ability to deal with multiple constituencies such as faculty, staff, students, prospective students, parents, counselors, media, regents, or board members
- Organizational ability
- Problem-solving orientation
- Ability to plan
- Ability to implement the plan
- Follow through
- Ability to write and speak well
- Ability to draw various campus units together in the common cause of greater student success on the campus
- Sense of humor

The listing is far from exhaustive. However, the traits listed above seem to be important to the successful implementation of an enrollment management plan on all types of campuses. There may be particular requirements for a given campus that will override some of those mentioned above.

The search for a chief enrollment management officer should be conducted at the highest level with input from faculty, students, senior staff, and the chief executive officer. Given the political complexity of most public university campuses, selecting an internal candidate may or may not avoid some of the difficulties of reconstituting existing portfolios. Political shifts of the magnitude required for this reorganization may unsettle even the most respected of the campus staff. Each campus will need to deal with the reality of their situation with regard to the search, selection, and organization process.

Admissions. In the public university the undergraduate admissions office most often comes under the aegis of enrollment management. On some campuses graduate admissions are part of the enrollment management portfolio. Since the admissions activities of the two divisions differ so dramatically, it may make sense to separate the graduate admissions function under the dean of graduate study or to have a separate director of graduate admissions who reports directly to the chief enrollment management officer.

At the undergraduate level, admissions is a combination of market research, student recruitment, and application processing activities. In the public setting, the admission processing section may be a separate unit. In keeping with the philosophy of total coordination of enrollment activities, it makes sense to include the entire admission effort under one director. This director takes on a large task but the elements of marketing, recruiting, and admission processing are so closely linked that the combination allows a more efficient blending of these functions.

The director of admissions position requires a combination of qualities that are rarely found in a single individual. Yet, it is vital for enrollment management that such a person be found. The qualities are:

- Intelligence
- Knowledge of market research techniques
- The ability to motivate people to do the very difficult work of admission recruiting and processing
- A high degree of managerial competence in order to combine the functions of the admission office described above
- The ability to represent the institution in a variety of settings with prospective students and parents, with faculty and alumni, with counselors and colleagues from other institutions.

The director of admissions will be one of the most visible people on the campus. He or she must be an eloquent spokesperson for the concept of enrollment management. The director of admissions is one of enrollment management's front line staff leaders. The director of admissions may often be called upon to substitute for the chief enrollment management officer when necessary.

Director of Financial Aid. The growing crisis in financial aid funding and the importance of providing the most accurate and up-to-date information on financial aid to all the enrollment management publics mentioned in the director of admissions position requires the financial aid director to possess a combination of technical expertise and a sophisticated and sensitive approach to management and public relations. This combination of abilities is also rare.

The modern financial aid office is a maze of electronic communications and data-processing equipment. Financial aid officers operate amid a growing bureaucratic tangle at the federal and state levels. They are often called upon to assist in the cultivation of donors who wish to designate gifts for scholarship purposes. They are also asked to make presentations to large groups of prospective students and parents. Staying abreast of the latest changes in financial aid distribution methodology and computer-assisted delivery technology is, in itself, a full-time job. In addition, the financial aid office must deal with walk-in counseling financial aid traffic of thousands of students per term at the large public university.

Identifying and nurturing a financial aid director who combines these abilities and interests is one of the most important jobs of the enrollment manager. Price setting and differential packaging of financial aid may be less important in the public university but the intricacies of state financial aid policy and university-wide distribution of scarce aid resources add a level of complexity to the job which requires great attention from the director.

The qualities which define the successful financial aid director are the following:

- Expertise in the computer-assisted delivery of financial aid information. This includes knowledge of such basic software systems and software vendors as Information Associates, SCT, Excellere, AMS, and others that enter the market with varying degrees of acceptance and success.
- Expertise in state and federal financial aid policy.
- Membership in the local, state, and national networks of financial aid professionals who make it their business to know the latest information from the state capital and the nation's capital.
- Involvement in the professional associations of financial aid officers. Not only do these organizations distribute information they also help influence state and national legislation which affects financial aid and its delivery. The effective director of financial assistance must be involved in this type of activity.
- A human quality which allows the director to work well with all types of students and to help the staff deal with the strain of working against some of the toughest deadlines in the business.
- A commitment to helping students but an understanding of the important role financial aid plays in the choice process of students and families. This is an extremely important area and should be thoroughly explored by the vice president for enrollment management and the director of financial assistance so that clear signals are established regarding priorities in setting up scholarship programs and the allocation of other types of aid and the delivery of financial aid information.

Retention

The natural affinity between recruitment and orientation is easy to see. The continuum of prospect identification, application for admission, acceptance, yield activity, and new student orientation is a natural one. Many enrollment managers now consider that the first year of college continues to be, at least in part, a function of continuing recruitment.

The merging of the two functions is not necessary. Indeed, there are enough dissimilarities that it is not practical for recruitment and orientation to be managed jointly, particularly at the public university. Yet, it is important for the orientation staff to be very much involved with the recruitment activities of the campus. They should have a hand in the design and writing of publications to ensure that the information conveyed to prospective students is current and accurate. They should also be involved in on-campus recruitment activities when students and parents are invited to the campus for special events. Orientation staff are trained to deal with the questions this group will ask. They are also trained to represent the campus positively and accurately. The recruitment office may be thankful for their help when the staff has been stretched thin due to travel or other commitments.

The orientation staff should involve the recruitment and registrar's staffs in planning for orientation. In the case of the registrar, it will be necessary since most orientation programs will contain some information or activity associated with course selection and registration.

Admission recruitment or outreach officers may also serve in important ways during orientation. Many of the new students and their parents will be well known to the admission officers since they have been in touch with one another throughout the admission process. At Riverside, the admission outreach staff conducts a series of summer orientation sessions in the homes of current parents or alumni. These sessions allow for questions and answers about the campus and provide an opportunity for current students to meet the incoming group and for the new students to meet one another and make plans to car pool, share rooms, or live together off campus.

Creating the Climate for Enrollment Management

It is very important for the enrollment management to understand the existing recruitment and retention efforts on campus and to blend new initiatives with those that have already demonstrated their effectiveness. Building a spirit of cooperation among all the units on campus which bear on recruiting and retention will be an important element in determining the ultimate success of the enrollment management program.

Natural lines of alliance will already exist. The enrollment management team will need to work very closely with the public relations office on campus. This will include the news service and the publications production team. Enrollment management requires quick response from the news media and the best available publications if the word of campus programs and activities is to be effectively conveyed to the many publics the campus wishes to reach.

The alumni affairs office is another natural ally for enrollment management. Building a relationship with this office will be crucial if the enrollment management wishes to develop an alumni admissions advisory committee to assist with recruitment. Alumni and parents of current or recent graduated students can extend the reach of the campus far beyond the capability of the professional staff.

The enrollment management must be able to discern these natural alliances and to build them where needed. The campus culture must be shifted in such a way that all those who come into contact with students realize the role they play in recruiting and retaining students. To build this culture, it is essential to encourage cooperation and pride in the campus. At the University of California at Riverside we convene a committee on the opening of school. This committee is comprised of people from every segment of campus life: orientation, physical plant, residence halls, academic advising, deans offices, registrar, admissions, financial aid, security, and dining halls. Each representative is asked to report on their state of preparedness for the influx of new students and to discuss any problems they foresee. The exchange of information is one of the best features of this type of committee.

**Goal Setting and Planning to Reach
Campus Enrollment Goals**

The goal of the campus enrollment plan may be to stabilize growth at an ideal level and then work to improve quality. More likely, it will be to grow to a certain level while at the same time improving student quality. At the public university, the enrollment goals, both near and long term, will be influenced by the ever present pressure of state legislatures on budget levels and the need to meet the requirements of the state plan for higher education. However, to the extent possible, each campus should have a basic enrollment plan which is agreed to by the major figures in campus planning, faculty, leaders, and senior staff. Once the goals have been clearly articulated, then constructing the plans which will move the campus in that direction may begin.

The enrollment management plan does not need to be an elaborate document detailing every step in the recruitment/ retention cycle. It does need to show that there is an understanding of the market elements which influence the campus' ability to meet the enrollment goal. If no market research has been conducted to determine the campus' market posture and position, such research should be undertaken at once. Market research does not have to be exhaustive or outrageously expensive. It should be well designed with great attention paid to proper sampling in order to get useable results. Litten (1977) has said that it is important to build trend data rather than take snapshots of the market position of a campus. Only by building the information base will you be able to understand how these trends are shaped and give you the information you need to position the campus for best response.

The plan itself is a document which sets targets and gives some sense of how the campus expects to reach these goals. The plans may include the commitment of the campus to increase the number of underrepresented ethnic minority students. For the public university this is a priority which must be at the top of the enrollment management agenda. As in all enrollment management models, retention is just as important as recruitment. The ability to hold and graduate the students who are recruited is central to the success of the overall efforts.

The plan should be general enough that it is easy to explain and to modify the account for shifts in the environment such as a change in the state economy or funding priority for higher education. The plan should include general statements about goals for each of the units in enrollment management. It should also outline how each unit will work toward internal goal setting and planning to help the campus achieve the overall goals.

The enrollment manager should not micromanage the units in enrollment management, but should broadly delegate authority to the directors and other managers to be as creative as possible in coming up with solutions and approaches that further the completion of the enrollment management mission.

Communication

The admonition to encourage the individual unit entrepreneurship does not remove the responsibility of senior management to build the team. The easiest way to do that is by consistent, timely, accurate communication with the enrollment management leadership. Regularly scheduled staff meetings and retreats will build that sense of shared responsibility and create a climate of loyalty and integrity which are absolutely essential if the enrollment goals are to be met.

Conclusion

Enrollment management is a concept which is still finding its way among higher education managers in America. The need to better organize recruitment and retention on America's largest campuses will soon have some variant of enrollment management located on virtually all public university campuses in the country. It may be called something else but the premise will be the same. At its best, enrollment management calls the campus together in an effort which is at the heart of success for any educational institution. It allows the campus to marshall its forces around the essence of the educational enterprise, the attraction of top scholars to our campuses, and the successful completion of the programs of study these scholars elect to pursue. Helping create institutions that allow this to happen is perhaps the highest calling any of us may heed. Let us do it joyfully and capably.

References

Hossler, D. (1984). *Enrollment management: An integrated approach.* New York: The College Board.

Ihlenfeldt, W. (1980). *Achieving optimal enrollments and tuition revenues.* San Francisco: Jossey-Bass Publisher.

Ingersoll, R.J. (1988). *The enrollment problem: Proven management techniques.* New York: Macmillan Publishing Company.

Litten, L.H. (1977). *Marketing higher education: A reappraisal in marketing in college admissions: A broadening of perspectives.* New York: The College Board.

Chapter 4

Minority Student Recruitment Issues in Managing Enrollments

Angela M. Roberson

One cannot authoritatively speak of managing enrollments for the future without having first established a comprehensive minority student recruitment and retention program. Projected demographic changes in the college-bound pool, different student characteristics, and special minority student interests and needs dictate the necessity to review minority student marketing, recruitment, financial assistance, counseling, and retention programs.

In this section, the need for a comprehensive minority student recruitment and retention strategy will be addressed. Discussion will focus on major components of a comprehensive minority student recruitment model, including recruiting for retention. Recommendations will be made to assist one in developing effective programs for increasing minorities' participation in higher education.

For the purpose of this section, minority students are identified as black or African-American, Hispanic, Native Americans, and Asian Americans. Most of the comments are directed toward issues concerning these students who are traditionally underrepresented in higher education.

Hodgkinson (1985) projected that by the year 2020 current trends indicate the following:

- The 14.6 million Hispanics in the United States will grow to 47 million
- The 26.5 million African-Americans in the United States will grow to 44 million
- A continuing decline in the birth rates of whites
- 34.3 percent of the United States population will be minority with most of the white population beyond the child-bearing years
- Increasing growth among Asian Americans largely due to current immigration patterns
- Minorities will span a broader socioeconomic range.

Other projections take into consideration the rash of children born to teenage mothers, the climbing increase in the percentage of children born into poverty, decline of approximately five million youth in the 18- to 24-year-old cohort, a continuing increase in the number of college graduates who will get a job which does not require a college degree, increasing numbers of talented minority youth selecting the military, and a major increase in college students who require both financial and academic assistance (Hodgkinson, 1985). The future also holds mounting numbers in the lower paying service jobs, single heads of households, and an increasingly diverse student population in terms of academic strengths, abilities, and needs (Hodgkinson, 1985).

These data seem to suggest that minorities will make up a larger portion of the pool of college-aged students. In all likelihood, a greater proportion of these students will be poor and many will come from single-parent homes. A large segment of this population will be at risk, both in terms of home and school environments. Students will bring increasingly diverse needs and interests to postsecondary study and careerism will continue strongly to influence college attendance. Further, it is likely that among these students, the value of higher education will be sorely tested in the years to come. Proof of its significance and effect in meeting one's goals will be demanded (State Higher Education Executive Officers, 1987).

As a consequence, one cannot simply ignore these trends

nor can enrollment managers fail to include these considerations in their planning for two major reasons. First, education is in a position to affect positive social change (State Higher Education Executive Officers, 1987). The belief that higher education is an "equalizing" factor continues to support many of our society's hopes and dreams.

"The nation's ability to compete is threatened by inadequate investment in our most important resource: people (Davenport, 1989)." By the year 2000, full use of the human capital represented by minorities will become increasingly critical (Davenport, 1989) and failure to address this urgency will be disastrous in terms of lost talents and perhaps social upheaval.

Second, the self-interest of the institution is critical to the enrollment of minorities to maintain or increase matriculants in the period of projected enrollment decline. The social and political ramifications of these trends are numerous and these issues need to be confronted and acted upon (State Higher Education Executive Officers, 1987). According to the State Higher Education Executive Officers (1987), "what is needed is a level of commitment that produces change so fundamental that the risk of retreat is forever banished." The required change benefits all minorities and all in U.S. society. Nonetheless, it would be grossly irresponsible for higher educators not to recognize and act upon the unique power and potential they have to make a significant difference in the lives of individuals and, by extension, the communities those individuals represent (State Higher Education Executive Officers, 1987).

In addressing the issues associated with institutional self-interest, the matter of institutional survival directly surfaces. Future enrollments, graduate achievement, alumni giving, and institutional image are factors that span the scope of enrollment management (Hossler, 1986). Therefore, declining enrollments, increasing poverty, and the implications for career preparation affect enrollment management. Minority student recruitment is not simply minorities' demand for equal opportunity; it enters and permeates the lives of all, affecting the welfare of the total society and the shape of higher education in the near future.

Constructing a Minority Student Recruitment Strategy

Recruiting and retaining minority students is one representative paradigm of enrollment management. All components of a successful minority student reruitment program intricately involve many enrollment management features. For the sake of achieving any progress in minority participation in higher education, recruitment and retention of minorities must go hand in hand. The following minority student recruitment model has as its primary feature "coupled" recruitment and retention, interchangeably contributing to the other's aspect of minority students' representation in higher education.

An additional component of an enrollment management system is the process of inter-relationships with many areas of the university community (Hossler, 1986). To ensure the quality of life, social and academic support systems, appropriate instruction input, and purposeful and practical policies, an institutional climate which would attract potentially successful minority students, ongoing cooperative collaboration, and effective communication are necessities and become essential elements for minority student retention.

A comprehensive minority student recruitment program has to be multifaceted to address a variety of needs and interests belonging to many "different" individuals of minority or ethnic backgrounds (Taylor, 1986). One minority's experiences can be totally different from another's although they both may have some common experiences. Therefore, addressing minority student needs can become a rather complex challenge. Utilizing one model of minority student recruitment can perhaps illustrate a few concrete examples of enrollment management in action. This model contains three major programs:

University-wide marketing strategies. These plans include the scheduled publications and mailings, school visitations, campus visit events, telemarketing programs, geographically-specific hotel receptions and interviews, financial assistance workshops, and their follow-up activities designed to attract and sustain the interest of all prospective students.

Specific recruitment activities targeted to meet minority students' needs. Designed to foster interest in science and technical fields underrepresented by minorities, this project will increase the number of black and Hispanic students enrolled. Funded through a foundation grant, this project supplements the university's effort providing monetary support specifically for its minority student recruitment activities. Some of these activities could include: special "tailored" campus visit events, minority schools counselor informational sessions, additional individual student/parent contact, local elementary minority student advising, and the publication and mailing of brochures related to the minority experience at the university. In the development of the above-mentioned programs, currently enrolled minority students, members of the Division of Student Affairs, faculty and administrators, and members of minority communities should be involved.

Academic and social preparation program for high school students. A project formed in partnership with the university, local community college, and a large community organization will bring many resources together to improve the academic and social preparation of minority students for participation in higher education. Three components of this type of project are viewed as providing continuity and offering a variety of experiences to assist students in becoming responsible for their own education and to better prepare them to meet the challenges of higher education. Those components are: an academic year of instruction, a summer residential session, and an internship.

Targeting minority high school freshmen, sophomores, or juniors, this program would offer instruction in science and technology fields taught by college and university professors, an SAT/ACT preparation course, guest lectures from professionals in science and technology, related field trips, and cultural activities.

Students would undergo a simulated college experience through an academic and social residential experience, interacting with currently enrolled minority students serving as role models and staff. A science and culturally-oriented weekend trip could be featured. This program is intentionally designed to heighten motivation and to address the effective domain associated with college attendance.

The project would culminate in a competitive internship. Paid internship positions at area hospitals, banking institutions, credit unions, realty companies, civic organizations, science laboratories, and various industries provide a meaningful work experience along with consistent professional intercommunication which adds to the encouragement many students need to attempt something "new and different."

Despite the many activities and details associated with the current model of minority student recruitment, the processes and philosophy of this model remain most critical to our discussion. This model is today's response to meeting the challenges that are now perceived to be in store for most universities.

The minority student recruitment process contains the following enrollment components which deserve special emphasis:

- Identifying desired student characteristics
- Analyzing admissions policies and practices
- Implementing specific recruitment efforts
- Developing financial assistance incentive
- Creating academic preparation assistance programs

Identification of
Desired Student Characteristics

A major component of enrollment management is the process or activity that helps shape the characteristics of a student body through marketing, recruitment, and admissions (Hossler, 1986). Minority student recruitment involves several activities based on a philosophy of providing the best opportunity for the student to achieve success. To provide the best opportunity, enrollment managers must determine the student characteristics necessary for the optimum match with the institution, including full consideration of institutional characteristics (Ayres & Bennett, 1983). This task is paramount to not only assuring a smooth transition into the collegiate environment, but is also essential in retaining students (Tinto & Wallace, 1986). The "institutional-student" fit is therefore most important in the creation of this opportunity.

Institutional characteristics pertain to the size, academic and social environment, instructional methodologies, and teaching quality, among other features affecting student achievement (Ayres & Bennett, 1983). Taking institutional characteristics into account, student characteristics are then determined which would allow the student to achieve both academically and socially. Such characteristics translate into the ability of the student to contribute to his or her learning and the ability of the student to contribute to the institution. Diversity through different cultural experiences, ethnic backgrounds, socioeconomic status, religious preferences, political views, and sexuality introduces "universality" into the university. Therefore, recruiting for a significant minority student enrollment deliberately shapes and forms the total student population.

Analysis of Admissions Policies and Practices

In recognizing and appreciating differences in students and in attempting to increase minority student representation, it is feasible that differences in admission policies and practices must be reflected. As cohorts, African-American and Hispanic students traditionally score lower on entrance examination scores. Seventy-five percent of African-American college-bound students had ACT composite scores of 15 or less (Cargile, 1984). In 1987–88, the national average ACT composite score for African-Americans was 13.6 and a mean composite score of 15.6 for Mexican-Americans/Chicanos and 17.0 mean composite score for people of Puerto Rican/Hispanic backgrounds compared to a mean composite of 19.5 for Caucasians (American College Testing Program, 1988). According to the September 12, 1989, national news release from The College Board, 1988–89 Scholastic Aptitude Test average entrance examination scores for minority groups when compared to an average verbal score of 446 and an average math score of 491 for white students were: 351 verbal and 386 math for African-American students; 381 verbal and 430 math for Mexican-

American students; 360 verbal and 406 math for Puerto Rican students; 389 verbal and 436 for other Hispanic students; 384 verbal and 428 for American Indian students; and 409 verbal and 525 math for Asian-American students. Per approximately 1 million bachelors degrees awarded in recent years, university graduation rates for African-American students have been approximately 6.5 percent and 2.4 percent for Hispanic students compared to over 83 percent for whites (American Council on Education, 1987). These figures show some rate of success on graduation surpassing the composite required by a number of institutions.

Whether the difference exists due to allegations of cultural bias in testing, of a lack of test-taking skills, or of testing experiences, the major premise here is that test scores are not the best predictors of graduation (Taylor, 1986; Trusheim & Crouse, 1984). Therefore, admission criteria must also reflect differences in minority groups' ability to succeed. In enrolling minorities, an admission policy must take into account a different weight or value for test scores.

In addition, other factors may need to be assigned different levels of importance as determined by institutional research which identifies the student characteristics which increase the predictability for success (Astin, 1982). Such factors may include quality high school preparation, past opportunities through which motivation was demonstrated, strong parental support and encouragement, school and community involvement, or a combination of these and other characteristics.

Implementation of Specific Recruitment Efforts
Strategies used in the recruitment of all students are of benefit in recruiting minority students. Typically, these strategies include: direct mail, college fairs, college day/night programs, high school visits, telephone calls, and campus visit programs. However, additional recruitment efforts are required to address the different needs, interests, and concerns of minority students (Lewis, Dorsey-Gaines & DeGarcia, 1989).

There are as many different needs, interests, and concerns as there are individuals. Counseling is essentially an "educative" process (Tinto & Wallace, 1986).

In helping students select the college/university that provides the best opportunity for full development, enrollment managers may enhance retention by decreasing the incidence of incorrect choices (Tinto & Wallace, 1986). By addressing retention (and recruitment) as an individual developmental task or process, institutions successfully facilitate minority students' academic, social, and personal development (Wright, 1987).

Minority student recruitment programs can take the form of housing community student groups on campus, bringing currently enrolled minority students to minority high school students, and developing special academic workshops in majors underrepresented by minorities. Telethons conducted by minority university students, introducing minority high school students to minority faculty and administrators, and hosting campus overnight visit programs strengthen the counseling that must take place. Involving minority high school students and their parents in these programs can assist in bringing counseling into the home and into the college decision process.

Development of Financial Assistance Incentives

If pricing is an important responsibility of enrollment managers (Hossler, 1986), then seemingly, so is assisting students and parents in determining if they can afford educational costs. Less federal money is now available for financial assistance than eight years ago and half of this nation's poor are children (Hodgkinson, 1985). Therefore, financing higher education has a tremendous impact on minority families especially as an apparent "underclass" begins to emerge—one in which it seems likely that many minorities will fall. Many of these students are uncomfortable with loans, having to assume a debt larger than their yearly family income (Arbecter, 1987).

Therefore, scholarships to minority students provide alternative means to assist the family in meeting direct costs to the institution. In addition, targeting minority student scholarships to both academic and/or need reinforces academic achievement and promotes the feeling of "belongingness."

Other strategies include packaging financial assistance to

offset loan dependency, creating financial aid models to reflect the different patterns of mobility for minorities, and strengthening the work portion of self-help. The perception of one's ability to afford higher education can be an especially acute issue among minorities as strongly implied by the large percentage of minorities in public versus private colleges and universities (American Council on Education, 1987).

Creation of Academic Preparation Assistance Programs

Academic underpreparedness is a major issue in discussions of minority student access to higher education (Astin, 1982). Whether the blame is attributed to the family, elementary schools, or secondary institutions, some students at all levels are found to lack academic preparation as determined by academic and skill deficiencies. In managing for the future, enrollment managers must seek to intervene, when possible, in the preparation of minority students for higher education. The suggestion is not to assume others' responsibilities; rather, it is an acceptance that special programs are needed.

In intervening, the enrollment manager contributes to improving the academic preparation among minorities. By the time students embark upon postsecondary education, they are more knowledgeable of what it takes to succeed and are, at the same time, more aware of their strengths and deficiencies. Through programs which provide guided assistance, students can learn to better use their strengths and to overcome their deficiencies. The intervention programs also provide additional counseling and marketing opportunities.

Any model designed to assist minority students to enhance their preparation for college should involve collaboration with minority community organizations, parents, school personnel, and other business or educational institutions. Encouragement and support should be widespread, coming from several sources at once.

Academic preparation programs can be instructional, tutorial, advisory, and experiential, involving various members of the university community. Instruction may be provided by college/university faculty and tutoring provided by currently enrolled students.

These situations have the potential for developing relationships with positive role models. Counselors and other university members can become involved in helping minority youth to better understand themselves, assess their own abilities and deficiencies, and take steps to further develop their skills and abilities. An experiential program potentially awakens in students heightened motivation, familiarity with educational practices, and a sense of personal achievement. Furthermore, programs such as these market higher education and career development as well as provide an essential link with minority student retention.

Enrollment managers contemplating developing minority students preparation programs should strongly consider designing these programs as early intervention tools. Although resources and budgets may be limited, attending to the needs of future freshman classes should logically produce some long-term gains for society as well as strengthen the prospective student pool. Minority students need to be "recruited" before they "mentally" or circumstantially drop out (Garza-Lubeck & Chavin, 1988). "We need to reassert the relevance of self-respect and high aspiration, and we have to persuade black youth that they can compete on equal terms not only in athletics and a few other circumscribed fields, but in fact across the whole spectrum of human striving—including the intellectual (Wharton, 1988)."

Recommendations for Program Success

Below are a few recommendations which the writer believes can make the difference between an adequate minority student recruitment program and a good program; a successful effort and a feeble attempt. These suggestions are directed to not only enrollment managers who have direct responsibility for program development and implementation, but also to those with whom the function of enrollment management lies.

1. Truly believe in the necessity for a comprehensive minority student recruitment and retention program. Enthusiasm needs to contagiously affect all faculty, administrators, and students who are concerned about the university being a viable institution of higher education in the years to come.

2. Transform the enthusiasm into real commitment. The commitment must be strong enough to survive shrinking budgets, personnel changes, and competing priorities. No longer can this commitment be subject to the whims of what is fashionable; it needs to remain a major strategy until there is no longer underrepresentation of minorities in all segments of society.

3. University resources must be rallied to provide support not only for the activities of enrollment managers, but also to support all areas impacted by increasing minority enrollments, whether it involves academic or social support services, hiring minority staff, funding scholarship programs, expanding relationships with minority communities—the allocation of resources must be viewed as permanent.

4. Actively listen to minority students, staff, and parents; seek the advice of minority community members and organizations; devise ways in which minorities become involved on all levels of the university's operation. Input from constituents can lead to an improved quality of campus life and a more effective recruitment and retention program.

5. Engage in extensive research. One must effectively know the targeted populations. Research concerning the demographics, access and retention issues, academic questions, special interests/needs, and obstacles is required. In learning to track the students who do enroll, one learns more about the specific students' characteristics which must be integrated into recruitment and retention strategies.

6. Openly work with colleagues from other institutions. Share the ingredients which make for successful programs. Together enter upon projects which can benefit minority students generally. Recognize major competitors and learn from them in order to strengthen one's own programs and services.

So much is at stake not only for minorities, but for all people; even those considered successful because of achievement in education and career. The political, economic, and social implications expand beyond today's issues. To delay action until the ramifications occur will force institutions of higher education into the proverbial "band-aid" mode of operation. Pro-active educational leadership is more than called for; it is the only option if education is to remain a true opportunity.

References

American College Testing Program (1988). *ACT high profile information.* Iowa City, IA: author.

American Council on Education (1987). *Minorities in higher education: Sixth annual status report.* Washington, D.C.: author.

Arbecter, S. (1987). Black enrollment. *Change,* 19(3), 14–19.

Astin, A. (1982). *Minorities in American education.* San Francisco: Jossey-Bass Publishers.

Ayres, Q.W., and Bennett, R.W. (1983). University characteristics and student achievement. *The Journal of Higher Education,* 54(5), 516–32.

Cargile, S. (1984). American College Testing Program Unpublished Report.

Davenport, L.F. (1989). The role of the community college in meeting Americans' future labor force needs. *American Association of Community and Junior Colleges (AACJC) Journal,* 59(4), 23–27.

Garza-Lubeck, M. and Chavin, F. N. (1988). The role of parent involvement in recruiting and retaining the Hispanic college student. *College and University,* 63(4), 310–22.

Hodgkinson, H.L. (1985). *All one system: Demographics of education—kindergarten through graduate school.* Washington, D. C.: Institute for Educational Leadership, Inc.

Hossler, D. (1986). *Enrollment management: An integrated approach.* New York: College Board Publications.

Lewis, B.J.; Dorsey-Gaines, C.; and DeGarcia, W. (1989). Personal contact strategies for minority recruitment. *The Journal of College Admissions,* 122, Winter.

State Higher Education Executive Officers (1987). *A difference of degrees: State initiatives to improve minority student achievement.* Report and recommendations of the state higher education executive officers task force on minority student achievement.

Taylor, C.A. (1986) *Effective ways to recruit and retain minority students.* Madison, WI: Praxis Republications, Inc.

Tinto, V., and Wallace, D.L. (1986). Retention: An admissions concern. *College and University,* 61(4).

Trusheim, D.W., and Crouse, J.H. (1984). The SAT and traditional prediction validity: A critical assessment. *The Journal of College Admissions,* 104, 9–12.

Wharton, Jr., C.R. (1988). *Public higher education and black Americans: Today's crisis, tomorrow's disaster? Minorities in public higher education: At a turning point.* Washington, D.C.: AASCU Press.

Wright, D.J. (ed.) (1987). *Responding to the needs of today's minority students. New directions for student services.* San Francisco: Jossey-Bass Publishers, 5–21.

Chapter 5

The Role of Financial Assistance Within an Enrollment Management Model

David Pardieck and Kathy Thomas

"Putting together individual aid packages for students is the final step in the student aid process, the narrow end of the funnel into which flow all the varied streams of aid. . . . Comparing every student's need and then dividing up the available grants, loans and work money in an equitable manner is an undertaking that might confound Solomon (Keppell, 1975)."

As the pool of prospective students has declined, and federal and state financial aid resources dwindle, it is natural that school administrators are increasingly concerned about the effective use of institutional aid resources. Therefore, the concept of bringing enrollment management practices to financial aid offices has rapidly gained support among university administrators and, thus, is changing the way many schools have traditionally awarded their financial aid.

Clearly, the role of financial assistance in the enrollment and retention of students has long been recognized. Numerous studies have been done which clearly demonstrate the impact of various financial policies and practices upon enrollment patterns (Elliot, 1980; Hearn, 1980). While these factors are conclusive and documented, many aid offices have continued to function in an operational vacuum, oblivious to the comprehensive enrollment goals of their schools and methods by which they can more efficiently and effectively influence student matriculation and retention. Hossler (1984) suggested, "Many financial aid officers resist using student assistance as a recruiting device; yet this is probably a key element of any enrollment strategy. To use student assistance effectively . . . the institution must develop . . . a philosophy of financial assistance for students."

It is generally easier to say than do something. The financial assistance office confronts, almost daily, a plethora of internally and externally imposed administrative burdens, generally leaving little time to develop the research base needed to develop effective and creative financial strategies and programs. However, if an institution is committed to controlling its enrollment patterns, the financial assistance office must become a key player on the enrollment management team. If this means allocating greater resources, both in staffing and operational support, then so be it. A college or university cannot be successful in its enrollment management efforts without a fully committed assistance office.

This chapter will discuss what we believe to be the fundamental aspects of financial assistance within an enrollment management model. These are some very basic but critical concepts and practices which must exist to successfully "market" financial aid. Since limitations of space preclude our detailing many aspects of institutional pricing and financial aid strategies, we will examine the four most important concepts:

- Differentiating the financial aid market segment(s)
- Strategies for market definition
- The need for variable or "target" packaging
- A plan for securing institutional resources

Finally, for the purpose of this chapter, we have further refined the definition of enrollment management, one which is operationally more accurate for financial aid. That definition is: supporting the attainment of the institution's enrollment goals through the efficient and effective use of financial resources. Or,

from a different perspective—maximizing desired enrollment
while minimizing financial aid expenditures.

The Marketing Environment

It is evident that the role of financial assistance is to provide
adequate resources to enable students to enroll in college.
However, to disburse resources without recognition of how
they will affect students' enrollment decisions is ineffective and
inefficient. The aid administrator must be aware of the various
factors which influence the enrollment decisions of the
institution's students and be able to recognize their differences.
In other words, the students who are influenced by financial aid
(major markets) need to be considered in light of their specific
characteristic difference (market segments). This is a deduc-
tive approach beginning with common factors evolving to more
specific considerations. The eventual goal of this market analysis is to specifically target available resources in a manner which
will generate the greatest return or "net" tuition dollar.

The various market characteristics that should be recognized
must be addressed by each institution. And, later in the chapter,
we will further discuss this process. However, before this
activity can begin, the institution must understand how students'
enrollment decisions are influenced by environmental and
pricing factors in the market.

There are many factors which enter into students' ability to
choose between various educational options, including the
students' academic strength (greater the ability, greater the
mobility), and student and family financial strength (Ihlenfeldt,
1980). The success of enrolling different types of students
depends upon the degree that these factors are considered in
the school's awarding model. The administration must review
the school's enrollment successes and failures in the context
of this variable. It may well be that the type of financial aid
package being offered is attractive to one segment of the
market, while a deterrent to another. For example, a packaging
philosophy based solely on financial need may not provide
adequate incentives for highly academically mobile applicants,

or those with a low computed but high perceived financial need.

At the applicant stage, institutional list price is significantly more important than the effect of financial aid, or the net cost (Elliot, 1980; The College Board, 1976). However, the evidence is clear that net price is a factor when selecting between two or more institutional choices (Hearn, 1980).

Therefore, equally critical to developing an effective packaging strategy is information about competitors and their award practices and resource allocations. Any financial aid administrator who is unaware of his competitors within the various market segments is not able to efficiently and effectively package financial assistance. One common mistake is assuming that financial assistance and admissions share the same competitors. While this may be the case, it is not necessarily so. Further, it is important to know how the competitor school is packaging assistance—level of need being met, distribution of assistance between gift aid and self-help forms of assistance, and offerings in academic and other talent-based awards. This information is critical to the development of targeted packaging. Without this data, only sheer luck will determine whether too many or too few resources are being expended within individual market segments.

Finally, an institution must analyze its own program(s) and determine their relative strengths in the market. The institution that finds itself offering a program or programs which may not be commonly available (either geographically or limited by number or quality or demand) must factor this variable into the awarding model.

Hossler (1984) summarized this critical need for institutional financial aid research: "Most admissions offices routinely collect data on each entering class. This information is usually transformed into an admissions profile of each class. Enrollment managers, however, also need to develop financial aid profiles of the student body . . . Clearly, there is a full agenda of research for enrollment managers in the area of tuition and financial aid."

Defining the Markets

The first step in defining markets is to understand their common characteristics. While it is inherently dangerous, considering the variety of institutional types to suggest what these factors may be, it is pretty much a given that the financial aid market includes all students who have a perceived and/or actual financial need, or perceive they have a special talent (academic, athletic, fine or performing arts) worthy of financial recognition.

The aid administrator (or enrollment manager) should define the segments of the institution's major markets. These would include the new student market (freshmen and transfers) and continuing (undergraduate and graduate) students. Of course, within these two major segments, there are at least two additional market segments. New students (freshmen) will have enrollment patterns different than transfer applicants. And, undergraduates will differ from their graduate/professional counterparts in decisions to continue their enrollment.

Any other characteristics of the major markets or segments should be differentiated in the awarding model in order to gain the maximum yield from each subgroup. Again, these factors are going to vary widely by institutional type. Only research can determine what factors are correct for each college or university. However, as a beginning, our experience has suggested the need to look at enrollment patterns among in-state versus out-of-state, various academic programs or majors, independent versus dependent applicants, ethnic and age groups, and levels of academic ability demonstrated by test scores and/or classroom performance.

Packaging Considerations

"Packaging is often referred to as the moment of truth for this is when the aid administrator combines all available resources and distributes them in a manner that will maximize access, choice and retention for the largest numbers of eligible students. This process is perhaps one of the most important factors in the whole chain of student aid delivery . . . (NASFAA, 1983, p. 1)."

With data provided through the market research, the aid administrator is able to bring enrollment management to fruition by designing a packaging model consistent with and supporting university enrollment goals. The packaging philosophy must target the major markets and segments and reflect the uniqueness of the institution. Within each segment, there must be the recognition of the students' mobility within the marketplace overlaid with data on program availability and characteristics of the competitor institutions.

An example may help to clarify this concept. An enrollment manager has done research into the enrolling patterns of his school's financial aid applicants. The data reveals that, when compared to overall applicant yield, those students with a high financial need and better than average rank-in-class tended to enroll at a less expensive competitor institution. Further research indicates that the primary reason for nonmatriculation was a real or perceived cost difference. In response to this problem, the school initiates a need-based scholarship which serves to increase the overall level of gift assistance in the financial aid packages of the higher ability applicants.

The financial aid packaging model must reflect all of the various factors which influence an institution's enrollment. They are the individual paints on the palette and the package is the finished picture. Each package should contain the correct distribution of gift assistance *vis-a-vis* loan and work programs. Further, the total assistance offered should be adequate to meet the institutionally determined need of each applicant.

Institutional Funding

"Rarely does a situation exist in which an institution has enough financial aid resources to meet the needs of its students. This fact coupled with recent reductions in federal and state aid make it essential for institutions to adequately plan for and monitor the resources they have (NASFAA, 1983, p. 3)."

Enrollment management within financial aid must include a

comprehensive program which provides for both short- and long-term planning, the monitoring of current resources, and the acquisition of additional resources of aid. This is essential to the future health and well being of the institution. Such an effort requires close coordination between the financial aid office and other affected departments at the institution. Annual review of the institution student funding situation will allow for necessary refinements and modifications in the overall aid plan.

Generally, financial aid offices have accepted the funding levels offered and then worked around the dollars with appropriate packaging policy. The result of this approach is that admission and marketing decisions often are delayed pending a funding decision. At best, decisions are made regarding enrollment strategy with the hopes that adequate funding will be realized. This reactive approach leads to overexpenditures of funding and last-minute modifications to the awarding model and is simply antithetical to positive enrollment management.

A better approach to this dilemma is to initiate an early market-sensitive financial aid budgeting process. This can be done most accurately if funding requests begin at the financial aid office level and then move upward. The process can be shortened if there is agreement at the front of a percentage range of institutional funding which will remain constant over a period of time. Budgeting processes vary greatly from one institution to the next. Public colleges and universities generally have a lesser degree of control over resource acquisition than their private counterparts. Therefore, the reality of the situation is that individual institutions may simply be unable to implement the procedure as detailed below. Ultimately, a successful enrollment strategy must include a market-sensitive financial aid budget.

The process must begin, first, as early as possible. The financial aid office should determine necessary levels of institutional funding. While estimates of need may be very broad, it is possible to establish a general range from which a request can be initiated. As the recruiting year progresses, the final funding will become firmer as variables in the projection become fixed.

Two variables must, by necessity, be established prior to projecting a funding level. First, the enrollment manager must determine minimum packaging requirements within an optimal enrollment model. This determination will require establishing the gap and packaging parameters which will assure adequate enrollment. Second, there should be an established benchmark for institutional funding levels which will remain relatively consistent from one year to the next. The benefit of the benchmark is that the packaging parameters can be established within reasonable funding limitations. For sake of example, this benchmark could be a figure such as 15 percent of anticipated tuition and fee revenue.

The resulting benefit of this request process will be that the packaging model will not have to be significantly changed as expectations in enrollment and other factors affecting funding begin to shift.

Summary

As institutions move toward greater integration of various campus units into a comprehensive enrollment management model, the role and perception of the financial assistance office will change. It will become evident that the policies and procedures for distributing financial resources must be scrutinized with regard to their impact on new enrollment and retention.

Without question, the prime directive must be to establish a research agenda, then use the data to formulate packaging policies which can assure the optimal net tuition dollar for the institution. But, balanced against the awareness of federal and other regulations intertwined with an overriding concern for fairness and equity, the effect will be both a challenge and a change for the financial aid professional.

Finally, who will do this critically important job? Probably the individual responsible for the day-to-day financial aid operation will not have the time to do this important work. Ideally, the institution should create or expand a position in which the individual will have the responsibility for research, strategy development, and program implementation. This individual must have the flexibility to develop the link between admissions and financial aid planning and operations.

References

College Board, The (1976). *Making it count: A report on a project to provide better information to students.* New York: College Entrance Examination Board.

Elliot, W.F. (1980). "Financial aid decisions and implications of market management." In *New directions for institutional research: The impact of student financial aid in institutions.* San Francisco: Jossey-Bass Publishers.

Hearn, J. (1980). "Effects on enrollment in student aid policies and programs." In *New directions for institutional research: The impact of student financial aid on institutions.* San Francisco: Jossey-Bass Publishers.

Hossler, D. (1984). *Enrollment management: An integrated approach.* New York: College Entrance Examination Board.

Ihlenfeldt, W. (1980). *Achieving optimal enrollments and tuition revenues.* San Francisco: Jossey-Bass Publishers.

Keppell, F. (1975). *Report of the national task force on student aid problems.* Washington, D.C.: U.S. Department of Education.

National Association of Student Financial Aid Administrators, (1983). *Standards for the development of policy guidelines for packaging need-based financial aid.* Washington, D.C.: NASFAA.

Chapter 6

The Role of a Career Center in Enrollment Management

Jane Linnenburger and Jim F. Vick

Securing a job upon graduation is a growing concern among college students and their parents. The success of an institution in placing graduates becomes an important consideration in selecting and persisting at a college. Career center participation in enrollment management "should not come as a surprise." There are obvious interrelationships with career planning and placement and all have an input on enrollments . . . (McConnell & Kaufman, 1984)."

There are two objectives for this chapter: first, to review some trends in the population and the work place that suggest the importance of a comprehensive career center in the enrollment management process; second, to describe practical program ideas and initiatives in three different aspects of enrollment management: attraction, retention, and renewal.

Trends in the Population

The pool of available high school graduates will decline from 277 million in 1987–88 to 245 million in 1993–94 with wide variations in state projections (McConnell & Kaufman, 1984). To stabilize or increase enrollments, many colleges and universities are seeking to recruit and retain more adult students. For

71

adult students choice of college is influenced by information on placement and salary potential, all of which is available through a career center.

Population demographics also indicate that between 1986 and 2000 the number of African-Americans in the work force will increase by 28.8 percent and the number of Hispanics by 74.4 percent (Riche, 1988). According to Cetron (1988), minorities will be the majorities in 53 of the 100 largest U.S. cities. The only growing segment of the traditional college market will be among the low-income and disadvantaged group, a group from which a small percentage of students normally attend college and an even smaller percentage graduate (Cetron, 1988). To maintain market share, and for other reasons as well, colleges and universities will have to attract and retain this population. The aggregate amount of loan indebtedness among this group is staggering and financial support from parents is minimal. In these cases student employment and cooperative education, essential parts of a comprehensive career center, are not merely attraction and retention factors, but absolutely necessary elements of a financial assistance program. Choice of college will even more be based upon these part-time employment opportunities.

These employment opportunities are critical, too, because of the rising cost of education. From 1976–86 the Consumer Price Index increased 96 percent, the cost of tuition 130 percent. The trend is expected to continue. Finally, even among traditional college freshmen, there is a greater concern about employment opportunities. *The American Freshmen: National Norms for Fall 1988* reports that freshmen are entering college to get a better job and to make more money (Astin, Green, Korn, Schailt, & Berz, 1988).

Trends in the Work Place

The work place has changed, too. Of all the new jobs that will be created over the 1984 to 2000 period, more than half will require some education beyond high school, and almost a third will be filled by college graduates (Johnston & Packer, 1987).

In addition, employers are demanding more than a degree from college graduates. They are interested in practical career-related experience and demonstrated skills.

Once employed, graduates will be expected to continue learning just to keep up with changes in the work place. "Between 2 and 3 percent of the nation's labor force, which is projected to reach about 135 million by the year 2000, may need to be retrained each year (*The Chronicle of Higher Education,* 1987)." It is estimated that business and industry already spend three to four times as much annually on training and retraining employees than is spent on all of higher education (Hodgkinson, 1986).

The message is clear—colleges and universities need to expand their offerings to meet the demand of the modern work place. To survive in the future, many educational institutions will have to change their view of education as neatly packaged three-credit hour courses designed by departmental curriculum committees. Many universities are already responding to this change by expanding continuing education offerings, establishing training centers, and developing contract learning programs in conjunction with business and industry. John W. Porter, former president of Eastern Michigan University, envisioned the Eastern Michigan of the 21st century as made up of 40,000 students, 20,000 involved in education contracted by the work place.

The career center with its network of contacts among employers, alumni, parents, and counselors is in an advantageous position to promote the university to these emerging markets. In light of these trends colleges and universities have become more aware of the need to package their career advisement and job search assistance not only to provide comprehensive career services through one's center, but also to assist in the enrollment management process. Some institutions have been successful in combining and strengthening programs through the establishment of comprehensive career centers which include career advisement, cooperative education, part-time employment, and placement services. The career centers attract the interest of prospective students as well as help retain enrolled students who can establish a relationship with the center as early as their freshman year and begin the career development process which will continue through graduation and beyond.

Career Center Programs
Related to Enrollment Management

The programs of a comprehensive career center related to enrollment management generally fall into three categories: attraction, retention, and renewal; although some programs obviously have impact in more than one area.

Programs under the category of attraction involve the production and dissemination of promotional brochures describing services, placement statistics and success stories, and the development of personal and multimedia presentations. These are directed primarily at high school and community college students, their parents and counselors, and, in large measure, are in support of existing admissions office efforts.

Retention programs primarily involve career advisement, cooperative education, and student employment. The existence of these opportunities certainly is incorporated into attraction brochures and presentations, but programs such as cooperative education keep students in school both by providing financial support and making their education more relevant (Korngold & Dube, 1982).

Programs that fall into the renewal category are perhaps a little more obscure if only because they are so uncommon. Students returning to school after raising a family and graduates already in the work place seeking additional education to change careers, to get promoted, or simply to keep up with technology are involved in renewal. Their incentive for continued education is clearly different than the majority of traditional students. These individuals are not typically recruited by admissions offices since many would not have established networks to reach them. A comprehensive career center becomes involved because of its unique access to employers as well as alumni and parents involved in career advisement and mentoring networks, all of whom are potential students of the university of the very near future. This access puts the career center in a position to establish linkages between academe and the work place that are indirectly but significantly related to enrollment management.

Attraction
There are many different methods that the career center can use to promote and describe its services to attract the interest of prospective students and their parents. A combination of oral presentations, printed literature, and multimedia productions can effectively convey pertinent information.

Oral Presentations
The career center staff can develop a presentation for prospective students which concentrates on the career services that students can use during their first or second year of college. It is important that the students be able to see the short- and long-term benefits of the services. It is also helpful to include placement statistics and some information about the kinds of job opportunities available to graduates from the institution. Presentations can be delivered effectively with the use of multimedia tools such as slide shows or videotapes which highlight key elements of the presentation.

Presentations by the career center staff should be included in all programs hosted on the campus for prospective students and their parents such as special visit days, weekend programs, and new student orientation. Since these presentations can be very time consuming for professional staff, student employees, particularly those involved in forensics, speech, theatre and communication, can be easily trained to deliver very effective career center presentations. Prospective students going through information-packed orientations or visits tend to remember very little detail, but will remember a positive impression created by an effective presenter.

Depending upon staff time and demand, the career center staff could be available to meet individually with prospective students and their parents who are visiting the campus. Appointments can be arranged by the admissions staff as needed.

These appointments focus on any concerns or questions of the parents and provide a perfect opportunity to share information about the career development process, cooperative education and the placement success of graduates in particular fields.

Printed Materials
It is important that the career center staff be willing to respond in a friendly and helpful manner to all requests from prospective students and their parents. Typically, parents of prospective students telephone or send letters requesting information about the placement success of graduates from certain major fields or more details about cooperative education. Prompt response to their inquiries is essential.

Brochures highlighting career opportunities, cooperative education, student employment, placement statistics, and other related information can be developed for prospective students and their parents. It is also important to work with university departments to develop appropriate career and placement information for inclusion in college catalogs, admissions viewbooks, financial aid newsletters, and departmental fact sheets. Direct mail can also be very useful in delivering career information to targeted groups of prospective students. Career preference and personal interest information available as part of the ACT test can be used to target mailings to incoming freshmen. Transfer students can be singled out to receive information on cooperative education.

Special Career Programs
Special career programs both on and off campus for high school and community college students, parents, and guidance counselors are an excellent means of attracting students. Symposia with break-out sessions and ample opportunity for discussion on subjects such as preparing to live and work in the 21st century or what's new in the work place, that feature successful alumni, local employers, former high school students, and university professional staff are very popular among high school students and their parents. Invariably a discussion produces questions about admission requirements and financial aid and provides excellent opportunities for attraction efforts.

*Career Center Interface with Enrollment Management
and Other University Personnel*
Another factor that cannot be overlooked is the relationship
between the career center and the enrollment management
staff. It is critical that the enrollment management staff have
current information about the services provided by the career
center. This would include career workshop calendars, lists of
employers hiring graduates, cooperative education and placement statistics and employment trends.

Because faculty and department heads are also very involved
in attracting new students, particularly talented and gifted
students, they need information about the career potential of
the graduates. Many universities publish comprehensive graduate placement reports which summarize by college and by
department how many graduates were employed or enrolled
in graduate school, and in what states or countries. Additional
information includes average salaries by major, lists of top
employers, employment trends, and some interpretive materials.

Retention
A comprehensive career center offers programming to serve
freshmen through seniors. Since most new students have a
basic understanding of the career services available to them, it
is important that the momentum keeps building. They need to
hear repeatedly what it is that the career center can do for them.
To create greater awareness and desire among students, an
advertising campaign can be implemented which includes
strategies to promote career services to each class from freshmen through seniors. At the University of California at San
Diego, the career services center focuses attention on freshmen to "nurture their perception of the center throughout
their college tenure" and offers "a more sophisticated advertising message" as students progress toward graduation (Dorsey,
1986).

Freshman-Year Programs
To reach freshmen, presentations can be made in freshman-
level classes and in freshman residence halls. Since the Indiana

Institute of Technology Placement Office started to give presentations during freshman orientation, they have reported greater involvement from freshmen in activities that will help them to be successful in a job search (Patton, 1988). Bradley Univer-sity's new University Experience course (discussed in Chapter 7) and Eastern Michigan University's ongoing orientation provide a perfect opportunity to start new college students in the career development process. In addition to actually experiencing the career center through a narrated tour, the students are provided with an overview of the center's services they can utilize immediately.

At many institutions there are optional career planning courses and courses with career development components taught by career center staff. Through these initiatives students learn the career paths available, the expectations of the work place, the employment outlook, and, in some cases, produce a working resume. Such initiatives help relate learning to the work place and keep students interested in their academic programs.

Career Counseling
Career counseling with underclass students can offer rewards for both the students and the career center. Through individual and small group advisement, relationships can be established which continue until graduation. As a part of career counseling, students are referred to other services which will also help them to identify interests and career goals such as interest inventories, computerized guidance systems, career planning courses, job search workshops, and cooperative education or internships. If students understand the relevance of their course work to their chosen career, they are more likely to persist. Career counseling helps students to be more prepared for the job search process and thus more successful in gaining employment upon graduation (Powell & Kirts, 1980).

Part-time Employment
According to Astin *et al.* (1988), 82.7 percent of entering freshmen plan to work while in college. Employment for college students can consist of part-time jobs in the community

or on campus, as well as career-related cooperative education or internship positions. In any case, these students earn money which helps cover college expenses while acquiring skills and experience that will help them to make better career decisions and be more marketable to employers.

Part-time employment has been shown to be a positive retention factor. "Having a campus job of less than 25 hours per week increases persistence ... and contrary to a common perception, part-time work correlates positively to persistence even during the freshman year (Lenning, Beal & Sauer, 1980)." The career center can serve as a clearinghouse for employment opportunities such as part-time jobs in the community and on campus (work-study and non work-study), summer internships, and other summer jobs. These jobs are posted in the career center and other campus locations, entered to computer networks and electronic bulletin boards, and otherwise advertised. Although many placement directors are not too excited about managing the student employment program, there are two significant advantages in addition to convenient access to the pool of college work-study students:

- Students are exposed to the career center relatively early in their college career
- Career center staff have the opportunity to promote cooperative education and advise students of the advantage of career-related work experience.

Cooperative Education and Internships
Research shows that cooperative education programs help to attract and retain students (Sowers, 1986; Korngold & Dube, 1982). Through cooperative education (co-op) and internships, students have the opportunity to integrate classroom theory with career-related paid work experience. Cooperative education positions typically are based upon multiple periods of full- or part-time study and employment in business, industry, government and nonprofit organizations while internships are typically one-time positions.

Students realize many benefits from participation in these kinds of experiences. Bradley University students who completed co-op assignments in the fall semester of 1988 ranked the following as the top five benefits of participation in cooperative education:

- Career-related work experience
- Earnings
- Job opportunities upon graduation
- Greater self-confidence
- Clarification of career goals

Co-op students at Eastern Michigan University listed as additional advantages: networking opportunities, transfer of classroom learning to the work place and unusual opportunities to attend seminars and participate in training. Similarly, a recent employer survey showed that the most meaningful asset in hiring college graduates was extensive work experience related to a company's business. Furthermore, Calvin (1988) suggested that "Graduates with work experience have a competitive edge . . . Companies are more comfortable hiring graduates with direct industry experience. Generally speaking, they are less risky hires requiring less initial training."

Graduate Placement Activities
With today's emphasis on getting a good job and making more money, college placement advisors should be experiencing increased demand for assistance. By the time students are seniors, they should be very familiar with the career center's programs and, it is hoped, many have a head start on the job search process. The career center can be a valuable resource by introducing prospective graduates to various types of employers through campus interviews, job fairs, job bulletins, employer directories, and mailing lists. Students who graduate and find good employment opportunities are likely to promote the university to their colleagues and friends and will look to their alma mater for new employees particularly if they feel they were assisted by the career center as students.

Special Minority Programs
To respond to the particular needs of minority students, some universities have developed career development activities in

coordination with minority student offices. Such programs include an overview of the career services available, motivational presentations by successful young minority alumni, an opportunity for informal discussion with employers in various fields, special workshops on interviewing and resume writing, and career or job fairs.

Linkages with Parents
Parents of current students can be actively involved with the career center through participation on parent career panels and parents' career information networks. At Bradley University, parent career panels are presented each year during Parents' Weekend to provide students and their parents with current career information. Parents, who are selected as panelists based on their area of expertise, serve on five different panels representing each of the academic colleges within the university. Parents' career information networks include parents who have offered to respond to students' questions about career fields, job opportunities, and other career-related questions. Parent participation is solicited during new student orientation.

Linkages with Campus Groups
Career centers are very actively involved with student organizations like the honors program, professional fraternities and sororities, and clubs associated with departmental majors. Adopt-a-group programs enhance that involvement by assigning specific professional staff to existing groups. Staff serve as advisors by ensuring that all attend occasional meetings and social events, and solicit the group's involvement in career center projects.

Linkages with Academic Departments
Career center involvement in retention initiatives is often indirect and the center's role at times somewhat delicate, but extremely important. Students are retained at a higher rate when they view their education as more relevant to their future and their career. It therefore becomes a major role of the career center's professional staff to serve as a pipeline for information

from the work place essential for curriculum development. In this regard, career centers should become actively involved in college and departmental advisory boards either by participation themselves, by recommending appropriate board members from among their employer contacts, or by hiring career center staff who can also serve as adjunct or part-time faculty. Additionally, department chairpersons or designated members of the faculty can represent each academic department as part of a career center faculty advisory board. The faculty liaison serves as the primary contact for the department and is on the mailing list to receive job postings, workshop flyers, and other materials to announce to faculty and students.

Linkages with the Work Place
Maintaining strong relations with the business community is paramount for the career center. Part of this initiative involves creating opportunities to link employers with faculty. These include faculty/employer lunches during recruiting season, career center providing speakers and presenters to academic classes and arranging tours of academic departments. Such contacts often lead to employer participation in classes, faculty visits to work sites (also a positive aspect of co-op), and part-time lecture appointments. An axiom of the Division of Marketing and Student Affairs at Eastern Michigan University is that: "People support what they help create." Involvement of employers encourages student hiring, and predisposes them to recommend the institution to friends. After all, they feel they are part of the program.

Renewal
Programs that fall into the renewal category involve students returning to school after raising a family, graduates already in the work place seeking additional education for advancement or career change or simply to keep up with technology. The U.S. Department of Labor ranks occupations by a specific set of skill criteria. "Jobs that are currently in the middle of the skill distribution will be least-skilled occupations of the future, and there will very few new jobs for the unskilled (Johnston &

Packer, 1987)." This shift will indeed bring individuals into the renewal process and career centers are in an ideal position to promote university programs that meet their needs.

Career centers have ongoing daily contact with thousands of employers through on-campus recruiting, job referral programs, job and career fairs, and student employment. All of these employers are potential students. Many career centers have alumni career advising networks. At Eastern Michigan University it is called the Huron Network, at Ball State the Cardinal Network, at Cleveland State the Cleveland Connection. Each of these network members, as well as their colleagues, are potential students, not only advisers to current students. Career center staff members frequently interface with parents at Career Days, Parents Association meetings, New Student Orientations, and Parent Career Panels. Each of these parents is a potential student, not just a parent of a potential student.

Individuals in these three groups: employers, alumni, and parents are potential students for traditional college courses as well as courses offered through continuing education or Colleges of Life Long Learning like that at Wayne State. More and more universities are developing innovative partnerships and training arrangements with business and industry that make the expertise of the faculty available to the work place.

Course content is defined by the customer. Eastern Michigan University has developed a Corporate Education Center with a championship 18-hole golf course and a 250-room Radisson Hotel. The technically advanced complex was built with both public and private funds and was designed to meet the educational needs of corporate America. The university created a new division entitled Corporate Services to meet the changing training and education needs of individuals and organizations by providing them with educational experiences tailor made to meet those needs. Corporate Services helps develop learning links with all sections of the community business and industry, government agencies, professional organizations, and elementary and secondary units of education. At some universities small business development centers have been developed to assist new and growing businesses and offer opportunities for faculty and student involvement.

As universities move toward these kinds of educational arrangements, the role of a career center in enrollment management will increase because the composition of the student body will change. Much of the career center effort in this area of renewal is a matter of broadening focus, recasting existing written material and acting as a distributor of information about these new university programs.

Many programs designed for current and prospective students such as career seminars done in high schools, orientation programs, and school visitations are attended by many parents, employers, and guidance counselors. These programs represent great opportunities to develop separate program tracks and to promote individual courses, specific faculty, or new programs that might be of interest to them. Most universities have some kind of visitation program. More often than not parents or other family members accompany their students. Separate programs are often designed for parents, providing a great opportunity to promote continuing education to them. Many recruiters and employers visit the career center annually. The focus is generally on providing students for them to interview. It is also a great opportunity to provide information packets about educational opportunities for them. That information, properly packaged, would be valuable not only to the recruiter, but to his or her colleagues in the work place.

Conclusion

The career center is an essential component of an enrollment management program. The functions performed by the career center have a significant impact on enrollment. This chapter demonstrates the many ways in which a career center is instrumental in attracting new students, how its program offerings encourage retention of current students and how its special linkages with external constituencies promote the renewal process.

References

Astin, A.W.; Green K.C.; Korn, W.S.; Schailt M.; and Berz, E.R. (1988). *The American freshman: National norms for fall 1988.* Los Angeles, CA: Higher Education Research Institute.

Calvin, B. (1988). Making the most of internships and co-ops. *NSBE Journal.* 4-2, 4.

Chronicle of Higher Education, The. (1987). Census Bureau Statistics, p. 33.

Cetron, M. (1988). Class of 2000. *The Futurist,* 22(6).

Dorsey, A.M. (1986). How to create a winning ad campaign for the career center. *Journal of Career Planning and Employment,* 49(2), 38–42.

Hodgkinson, H. (1986). Guess who's coming to work. Columbus, Ohio: National Center for Research in Vocational Education, Ohio State University. Occasional Paper No. 116.

Johnston, W.B., and Packer, A.E. (1987). *Workforce 2000.* Indianapolis, Indiana: Hudson Institute, Inc.

Korngold, A., and Dube, P. (1982). An assessment model for cooperative education program planning, management, and marketing. *The Journal of Cooperative Education,* 19(1), 70–82.

Lenning, O.T.; Beal, P.E.; and Sauer, K. (1980). *Retention and attrition: Evidence for action and research.* Boulder, Colorado: NCHEMS.

McConnell, W.R., and Kaufman, N. (1984). *High school graduates and projections for the fifty states (1982–2000).* Boulder, Colorado: Western Interstate Commission for Higher Education.

Patton, P. (1988). The placement office has a place in freshman orientation. *Journal of Career Planning and Employment,* 48(2), 20–21.

Powell, C.R., and Kirts, D.K. (1980). *Career services today.* Bethlehem, Pennsylvania: The College Placement Council, Inc.

Riche, M.F. (1988). America's new workers. *American Demographics,* 10(2), 34–41.

Sowers, G. (1986). How cooperative education affects recruitment and retention. *Journal of Cooperative Education,* 33(3), 72–78.

Chapter 7

A Theoretical and Practical Guide to Student Development Programs in Enrollment Management

Ray K. Zarvell, Marlene Kuskie, Robert Bertram, Lee Noel, Randi Levitz, and Nancy Jones

When we use the term *enrollment management,* we are refer-ring to a complex interaction of elements. The term encom-passes everything from marketing to recruiting to admissions to retention. This chapter will emphasize the latter, focusing specifically on student development programs as the prime means to improving student retention.

Good retention practice ought to precede an institution's efforts to attract and enroll students. Institutions that have the most desirable and longest-lasting enrollment results are those that understand that structuring a climate of student success on campus (which in itself leads to increased retention rates) makes it far easier to recruit and enroll new students in the future.

The most effective way of addressing student retention is not through trial and error, nor knee jerk reactions, nor through efforts that might be characterized as hit-or-miss. Rather, it is to analyze the factors that contribute to attrition and to counter these factors with purposive efforts that have already proven themselves successful at reducing drop-out rates, or that promise a high likelihood of doing so.

To arrive at the factors that contribute to students dropping out of school, and to arrive at what we might call the "antidotes" to attrition, we can turn to one of two sources. First, we can look to the theoretical models that provide the foundation of research into enrollment management. These models offer us a basis both for investigating the problem at a given institution, and for pointing the way toward a solution.

The second direction we might take is to listen to the examples that use the theory, the success stories of given institutions. Taking this approach will yield "living" illustrations, as it were, which offer proof that enrollment management works. To understand why it works, however, it is important to return to the theories. And to understand how specific examples of success might be adapted to another institution, it is also important to return to the theoretical framework to encounter the broad range of possibilities that exist.

In the area of retention management, one of the most useful models for understanding the forces of attrition is Spady's (1970) early retention model, and, later, Tinto's (1975) conceptual schema. This approach identifies internal and external factors which influence an individual's decision to remain in a particular institution or to leave. Centering on several components that reflect the broad purview of student affairs, this model includes such factors as "social integration," "academic potential," "grade performance," "peer-group interactions," and other affective factors.

Complementing Tinto's theoretical framework is the model supplied by Noel and Levitz. First described by Noel, Levitz, and Saluri (1986), and developed more fully recently (Levitz and Noel, 1989), Noel and Levitz identify seven factors which have a primary bearing on a student's decision to leave school:

- Academic boredom
- Academic underpreparedness
- Uncertainty about major or career
- Difficulties with transition to college/university and adjustment to the institution
- Limited and/or unrealistic expectations of college
- Dissonance or incompatibility between the student and the institution
- Perception that the education they are receiving is irrelevant

Beginning with this schema, it is possible to develop a matrix identifying points of identification and institutional intervention (see Table 1). Points of identification range from specific cues observed or patterns uncovered for individuals to data gathered systematically on students across campus. Accompanying interventions are remedies for the themes of attrition and represent significant programmatic thrusts designed by the institution. Such a matrix (see Table 1) can guide an institution in its understanding of the tasks and programs necessary to support an effective retention effort.

As the matrix in Table 1 shows, the programs that figure most prominently in retention efforts are student orientation, academic advising, and counseling services. It is with good reason that these areas have been central to the actions of colleges and universities in countering the forces of attrition.

Orientation

Retention research has consistently indicated the freshman year as the point at which the greatest number of students are at risk of dropping out (Bean, 1980; Fetters, 1977). With this knowledge, an institution's orientation program is a critical time to identify and initiate work with students who may not possess the necessary skills to succeed at college.

Precollege academic achievement and aptitude variables have been shown to be useful predictors of persistence (Nelson, Scott & Bryan, 1984). Orientation provides an ideal opportunity for an institution to verify the abilities and aptitudes of incom-

Table 1
Attrition Themes and Resultant Points of Identification and Intervention

Theme	Institutional Means of Identification	Institutional Intervention
Academic Boredom	Large discrepancy between first-term grades earned and academic ability at point of entry; discussions with advisor; student's assessment of the academic advice they have received; student opinion survey	Academic advising; selection of more appropriate class placement based on student skill assessment; selection of other instructors
Academic Under-preparedness	Assessment of reading and other academic levels; prior achievement	Appropriate course ability placement; academic study skills training, counseling, academic advising; orientation
Uncertainty about Career	Senior goals and freshman applicant surveys; student opinion survey; discussions with advisor or teacher	Career and academic advising
Transition and Adjustment Difficulties	Comparison of non-matriculating and entering freshman surveys; student opinion classes; survey; discussions with counseling advisor or teacher	Orientation and freshman experience
Unrealistic Expectations	Student opinion survey; discussions with advisor, teachers, resident assistants	Orientation; freshman experience classes, advising and counseling
Dissonance or Incompatibility	Student opinion survey; discussion with advisor, teachers, resident assistant	Counseling; freshman experience courses; academic advising
Irrelevance of Education	Student opinion surveys; discussions with advisor, teachers	Counseling and exit interviews; academic advising

ing students to locate those who are prone to drop out. For example, reading test scores have been shown to be related to both academic performance and retention (Carney & Geis, 1981). Appropriate diagnostic tests along with individual advisor appointments can be effective in identifying students who may be at risk. Referrals can then be made to courses or services addressing the improvement of reading skills, effective note-taking methods, and time management techniques.

Such individual meetings with academic advisors, faculty, or administrators can be beneficial in focusing on specific transition and adjustment issues that may impede a student's progress. This may cause a dilemma of sheer numbers, of course, and might appear to be unmanageable. One solution is to invite students to campus in small groups throughout the summer and to rely on trained peer counselors.

It is also important that during orientation students begin to feel affiliated with the institution. A student's sense of their own social integration has been shown to be related to persistence (Astin, 1975; Nelson, Scott & Bryan, 1984; Pascarella & Terenzini, 1979). An example of institutional programming designed to encourage active social interaction has been demonstrated at Bradley University where computer software, Com-Link, has been developed. Students register their interests through an 85-item survey (interactive with the computer). The data are then applied to one or more of three menu items that match the students' interests, including: (a) clubs and organizations, (b) academic majors, and (c) on-campus recruiters who employ students of particular majors and interest. Used during orientation, this program becomes both an instrument for facilitating social affiliation and an instrument with which to begin academic and career advisement.

Helping students to understand the reason for general education requirements and the importance of a liberal education obviously adds to the student's understanding of the relevance of a college education. This educational process should also begin at orientation.

As discussed later in this chapter, academic boredom has also been identified as an attrition theme (Noel *et al.,* 1986).

Placement testing in areas where students may demonstrate a wide range of abilities, such as mathematics, chemistry, or foreign language, can provide academic advisors with data for accurate placement.

Academic Advisement

Students bring to institutions a variety of developmental concerns. For many students declaring an academic major can be a significant challenge. Some students choose to explore as many possible majors as available and refrain from a final decision for some period of time. These students, commonly called "undecided," have historically been an attrition-prone group. Many students who leave a university during their freshman or sophomore year do so without having developed any sort of career plans (Bradley & Wark, 1984). Students often report feeling lost at institutions geared toward students with declared majors. As Mable and DeCoster (1981) report,

"... much is left to chance as students struggle to meet the right people and establish confidence in themselves and their ideas ... [students] fear being trapped; ambivalent in their searching; and, most frequently they lack knowledge, information and decision-making skills (p. 9).

As a consequence, programs specifically designed to meet the developmental needs of undecided students can be advantageous for both the student and the institution.

One such program is Bradley University's Academic Exploration Program (AEP). The program expands the usual scope of academic advisement and focuses on three areas: academic, diagnostic, and career.

The academic element contains a complement of faculty from all areas of the university to advise students. Advisees are assigned to faculty based upon similar interest patterns. This proves to be a significant factor in increasing student satisfaction levels.

The diagnostic stage seeks to analyze student ability levels, interest patterns, and personality traits in an attempt to match the student with career and academic major interests that are challenging and appropriate. AEP students who participate in the diagnostic stage indicate this component to be a significant factor in academic major selection.

The career component begins with a noncredit course called the Student Planning Seminar. The purpose of the course is not to have the student select a major, but to ensure that adequate progress is being made toward major selection. The course allows the student to identify, as well as expand, his or her interests.

Other career components include the Footsteps Program. This program seeks to place students in the community for one day in a career field they are considering. This experience often emphasizes the relevancy of the student's course work.

Counseling Services

The counseling services of a university have been identified as a significant retention strategy (Kemerer, Balderidge & Green, 1982; Noel *et al.*, 1986). Further justification of this postulate is the correlation between the purpose of counseling and the Noel and Levitz retention themes of "dissonance and incompatibility" and "transition and adjustment difficulties." The quality and content of the counseling services must meet not only the institution's mission, but also be designed to be congruent with the developmental needs of the students it serves. After appropriate research and needs assessment have been conducted to identify potential attrition-prone students, programs need to be developed accordingly on a long-range plan.

While counseling encourages the growth of multiplistic thinking for better decision making, a variety of experiences and learning must occur for this to happen. Consequently, any help a counseling center offers to a student must have a component that meets immediate needs of the student for resolving problems.

Due to the developmental needs of attrition-prone students, much counseling is on a crisis basis with the desired outcome being immediate resolution of the problem desired. A brief strategic therapy model (DeShazer, 1985; Haly, 1976) is conducive to the average 3–5 sessions that occur in a counseling center whether or not the student is attrition-prone.

The brief therapy model encourages a contract for measurable, achievable behavior change to occur immediately in the student, while simultaneously changing the student's view of reality. Immediate remediation of the problem at hand and the student's success in making decisions is necessary to reduce attrition.

In addition, a holistic or wellness approach to counseling is indicated by recent research (Astin, 1988). In this research, Astin identified stress as a significant factor in student life. The counseling center serves as a resource to the campus in assessing, remediating, and educating concerning stress.

To be effective in the holistic/wellness component of the center, a strong working relationship with other services and the academic community needs to exist. Of primary importance is the relationship between residential life and the counseling center, for it is through residential life that education programs are presented and referrals are made before a crisis situation occurs. Such programming—on topics including time management, substance abuse, eating disorders, anxiety, and other wellness issues—encourages a strong relationship between students and counselors. Visibility and availability within the residence halls is being identified as a significant variable of meeting special needs of students (Deters, 1988).

Academic Success Program
The holistic/wellness and brief therapy approach as described previously might be a central component of an academic probation student program operating within the counseling center. For an academic probation program to be effective, immediate contact must be made with the student. A letter describing the services sent with the notification of the students' probationary status is more effective than communication received after the fact. Individual interviews need to be arranged as soon as possible so that the counselor and the student can assess the problem(s) and determine possible campus resources and begin intervention strategies. Many of the issues can be talked

about in a group setting, but the on-campus, one-on-one relationship between the counselor and student is more conducive to immediate behavior change.

After one to three individual sessions have occurred, approximately five seminars may be presented on a weekly basis that address the identified concerns. Topics for such seminars might include time management, assertiveness and student rights, motivation and procrastination, test anxiety and stress reduction, and eliminating self-defeating behaviors. Concurrently, individual sessions may be arranged but most interaction with the counselor comes through the seminar sessions. The program serves as an adjunct to other learning assistance programs by providing the social/emotional component to behavior change. Again, all aspects of student life are attended to in an academic success program through a cognitive/behavioral model.

Exit/Withdrawal Interview

A crisis intervention strategy to retain students is the withdrawal interview conducted by a counselor in the counseling center (Lenning, Beal & Sauer, 1980). All students making a formal withdrawal from the university are referred to the counseling center for the paper work, but more importantly to assess the conditions of the decision to withdraw. Such a process also allows the university to research reasons for attrition for future programing needs (Lenning, Beal & Sauer, 1980).

The purpose of the withdrawal interview is to re-evaluate the decision to withdraw and to ensure that all campus resources have been exhausted. Often the thinking process of the attrition-prone student is an either/or process. The decision is based on inadequate information or an inability to consider all options. The goal of the exit interview is not to convince the student to remain; rather, it is to work jointly with the student to seek directions for the student's potential success and happiness based upon the cognitive and affective information exposed during the interview. Again, a holistic approach is used in assessment so that all options and concerns are evaluated.

To be effective, the counseling center must discern needs, approach the student holistically, and have a strong developmental philosophy that encourages growth in behavior and cognitive areas through a supportive, trusting relationship. This goal is most efficiently reached through a brief therapy model with educative programs that expand the awareness of students to enhance their development. Through experiential awareness, a student's ability to make decisions is enhanced and student retention rates are positively affected.

Making the Connections Among Orientation, Advising, and Counseling

Getting students started right on the path to success in college is key to increasing a campus's retention rate. It is for that reason that programs such as those mentioned above—orientation, advising, and counseling—are important. Particularly in the opening weeks of a student's time on campus, an institution has a unique opportunity to take active steps to identify students at highest risk of dropping out, and to begin to put into place interventions that will counter these forces of attrition.

As can be seen in the models referred to in the beginning of this chapter, the decision to leave college is a result of a combination of complex underlying factors. Because these factors operate often below the surface, an institution must take active steps to identify or recognize signs that a student may be at high risk of dropping out, and put into place interventions prior to the student's reaching a final decision to leave.

Coming out of the work of Noel and Levitz is a retention management system that allows this kind of early identification. Such identification affords colleges with the opportunity to initiate early intervention efforts with students for whom the institution has appropriate programs and services. This type of early-alert system, which both identifies students to target for specific intervention and also guides institutional interaction, might be seen as a transcending activity or as a link between all the individual means of institutional identification described in Table 1 and elaborated more extensively in the previous sections of this chapter.

Efforts to improve student persistence must focus on helping freshmen make the academic, personal, and social adjustment to college. As Levitz and Noel (1989) have said, in order to make the "freshman connection," institutions must devise programs and services that will help the student

- connect to the environment
- make the transition to college
- work toward their goals in terms of academic major, degree and career
- succeed in the classroom

It was to aid colleges and universities in this effort that Noel/ Levitz Centers sponsored the development of the Retention Management System™, of which the College Student Inventory™ is the central component.

The College Student Inventory (CSI) was designed to provide insights into specific forces and factors that may lead a particular student to drop out of college. It was also designed to enable the college to tailor an intervention plan to meet each student's most pressing needs. Intended to be used during summer or early-fall orientation, the College Student Inventory assesses an extensive variety of dimensions related to dropping out of college. In the process, it provides extensive information about each student's academic and social motivation, identifying students at greatest risk of dropping out, and identifying which students will most likely be receptive to institutional intervention.

The information derived from this instrument gives the advisor or counselor a very useful set of insights into the deeper motives lying behind a student's general dropout tendency.

As Tinto has described, both academic and social factors are key in determining a student's motivational patterns. Using his schema as a springboard (see Figure 1 above), the College Student Inventory examines this motivational pattern in the academic realm through an assessment of a student's study habits, intellectual interest, academic confidence, desire to finish college, and general attitude toward education. Similarly, it examines student's social motivational patterns through an assessment of self-reliance, sociability, and leadership.

Additional understanding of a student's general coping ability is provided by the CSI through an assessment of family emotional support, openness, career planning maturity, their ease of transition, and sense of financial security.

Finally, a student's receptivity to support services gauges the extent to which the student will permit the institution to intervene on their behalf in the following areas: academic assistance, personal counseling, social enhancement, and career counseling.

This tool helps practitioners translate Tinto's theoretical approach to the study of drop-out behavior into an effective pattern of institutional intervention. Used in conjunction with an ongoing orientation program, the College Student Inventory can provide the institution with a regular and systematic way of tapping into the needs of students and providing them with assistance at the time when their need is most prominent.

While orientation provides an initial point of contact between the student and the institution, student advisors provide the ongoing connection and lifeline with the institution. They have vital responsibilities beyond helping students select courses and giving preliminary advice regarding career planning and academic development. They truly aid in a student's academic and social development on campus.

Orientation and advising, therefore, should work hand in hand. But there is a key problem in the way these usually come together. The advisor starts with so little information about a student. It is often the case that only a transcript is available. From that one can determine a student's history of academic performance, which is very helpful in predicting college success. But to do an effective job, the advisor needs to know how the student feels about school, how motivated the student is about studying, how committed to getting a degree. The advisor also needs to know what help the student wants, and what motivational blocks may hinder the student's progress.

It is at this point that an early-identification and targeted intervention system is most critical. And it is at this point that tools such as the Retention Management System's College Student Inventory can provide significant insight and guidance.

Institutional Structures Aiding
Retention Efforts

Motivated by declining enrollments, many institutions have designated directors of retention, some of whom occupy autonomous offices distinct from colleagues in either the academic or student affairs divisions of their institutions. A more innovative structure—and sometimes a more effective one—meshes into one unit responsibilities sometimes separated into either academic or student affairs. This unit is characterized by a vision of total integrated student development, linking such programs and responsibilities as orientation, academic advising, assessment testing and course placement, counseling, learning assistance and tutoring, and related student development programming areas.

This unified structure takes hold on campuses where academic and student affairs have equal respect and a common goal—that of student growth and student success. While retention is the responsibility of everyone on campus, everyone cannot be responsible for program design and delivery. Therefore, some division or unit such as that described above must provide the guidance while broadening ownership for these goals and activities campuswide.

Retention Research

The primary objectives of the efforts that have been described earlier in this chapter are to increase the rates of student success and student persistence on campus. To determine whether these objectives have been met, colleges and universities must also put into place a systematic approach to evaluate the effectiveness of these efforts.

Noel, Levitz, and Saluri (1986) have defined objectives for a comprehensive retention research program that will enable an institution to determine whether their retention efforts are making a difference. These include the following:

- To study success—to find out what the institution is doing well in order that it may do more of it

- To pinpoint campus programs and services that need further attention so they may become the type of student resources of which the institution can be proud
- To determine the type of intervention programs and practices that are linked to student success and student persistence
- To follow those students who receive special attention or participate in special programs to determine whether these interventions are having the desired impact
- To target students who will benefit from interventions known to have a positive impact
- To provide validation of the outcomes the institution is striving to achieve (Noel *et al.,* 1986, p. 350).

The activities listed in the matrix of Table 1 provide much of the data needed to meet the objectives of the retention research program listed above. These data provide key information for decision making concerning program design, delivery, and modification.

For example, student opinion surveys that highlight student satisfaction with the academic climate and offerings on campus shed light on academic advising, quality of freshman teaching, and the student-centeredness of the campus environment as perceived by the most important customer—the student. These help to identify institutional strengths to be built upon and performance gaps to be remedied.

Ultimately, effective retention research is much more than just taking periodic head counts and determining who, when, and how many have dropped out. Retention research is a comprehensive approach to increasing institutional effectiveness, for retention is a critical performance outcome indicator for the institution as a whole. If an institution is healthy, retention rates are high. And that, of course, is what every institution hopes for.

References

Astin, A. (1975). *Preventing students from dropping out.* San Francisco: Jossey-Bass Publisher.

Astin, A. (1988). *1988 freshmen survey results/cooperative institutional research program.* Los Angeles: University of California.

Bean, J.P. (1980). Dropouts and turnover: The synthesis and test of a causal model of student attrition. *Research in Higher Education,* 12, 155–87.

Bradley, L., and Wark, L.K. (1984). Career indecision: A dilemma and a solution. *NACADA Journal,* 4(1), 23–27.

Carney, M., and Geis, L. (1981). Reading ability, academic performance, and college attrition. *Journal of College Student Personnel,* March, 100–06.

DeShazer, S. (1985). *Keys to solution in brief therapy.* New York: Norton and Co.

Deters, K. (1988).Counselors in residence.*National On-Campus Report,* 44, 1–2.

Fetters, W.B. (1977). National longitudinal study: Withdrawal from institutions of higher education. Washington, D.C.: National Center for Education Statistics. (ERIC Document Reproduction Service, No. ED 150 913).

Haley, J. (1976). *Problem-solving therapy.* New York: Harper and Co.

Kemerer, F.; Baldridge, V.; and Green, K. (1982). *Strategies for effective enrollment management.* Washington, D.C.: American Association of State Colleges and Universities.

Lenning, O.; Beal, P.; and Sauer, K. (1980). *Retention and attrition: Evidence for action and research.* Boulder, Colorado: National Center for Higher Education Management Systems.

Levitz, R., and Noel, L. (1989). "Making the freshman connection: The key to student success and persistence." In M.L. Upcraft, J. Gardner and Associates, *The Freshman Year Experience.* San Francisco: Jossey-Bass Publisher.

Mable, P., and DeCoster, D.A. (1981). *Academic experiences and career orientations.* San Francisco: Jossey-Bass Publishers.

Nelson, R.B.; Scott, T.B.; and Bryan, W.A. (1984). Precollege characteristics and early college experiences as predictors of freshman year persistence. *Journal of College Student Personnel,* January (2), 50–54.

Noel, L.; Levitz, R.; Saluri, D.; and Associates (1986). *Increasing student retention.* San Francisco: Jossey-Bass Publishers.

Parscarella, E.T., and Terenzini, P.J. (1979). Interaction effects in Spady's and Tinto's conceptual models of college dropout. *Sociology of Education,* 52, 197–210.

Spady, W. (1970). Dropouts from higher education: An interdisciplinary review and synthesis. *Interchange* 1, 64–85.

Tinto, V. (1975). Dropout from higher education: A theoretical synthesis of recent research. *Review of Educational Research* 45(1), 89–125.

Chapter 8

The Role of Cocurricular Activities and Residential Life in University-Wide Enrollment Management

Greg Killoran and Ed King

Any attempt to explain the role that cocurricular programs can or should play in an institution's enrollment management system requires a conceptual understanding of enrollment management as well as a description of what comprises cocurricular programs.

An examination of a concise definition of enrollment management (Hossler, 1984) and ensuing explanations of its implications for institutions of higher learning suggest that cocurricular programs should play a part in the process. Hossler (1984, 1986) included student services as a significant contributor to enrollment management and indicated the need for university administrators to develop a new perspective "to view the students as well as the institution (Hossler, 1986)."

Hossler's statements issue a very challenging assignment to enrollment managers and suggest that the accomplishment of this goal will require the contributions of many and varied sectors of the campus community. As a component of the student services area, what are the expectations for cocurricular programs in the enrollment management process?

Before addressing this question, clarification of the term cocurricular is required. As pointed out by Frederick (1959), many names and phrases have been utilized to describe what is now referred to as cocurricular. Among others, he cited extercurricular, student activities, "the third curriculum," and even cocurricular. Whatever the terminology, this area encompasses those programs, activities, and organizations in which students participate outside the classroom. Is it realistic to hope that a collection of student activities programs are actually going to affect enrollment?

To Hossler (1984), enrollment management is viewed as being "concerned with student enrollments from the time of the critical inquiry through graduation and postgraduation." This seems to suggest viewing the student in three phases: as a prospective student, an enrolled student, and as an alumnus or in the recruitment, retention, and alumni relations stages. Can cocurricular programs, to include a myriad of student organizations and activities, intramural sports programs, recreational facilities, and student services for minorities and international students, positively affect recruitment, retention, and alumni relations? This chapter presents an affirmative response to this question and illustrates how and when cocurricular programs can contribute to the enrollment management process.

Much of what cocurricular programs do to affect enrollment happens naturally and does not require special attention from enrollment managers. This is fortunate because it is obvious that many institutions do little that could accurately be described as enrollment management. Further, many who claim to be involved in enrollment management processes have not focused their enrollment management lens wide enough. If it is true, as Hossler (1984) wrote that few institutions include financial aid in their system and that even fewer have developed retention efforts, then it seems reasonable to assume that fewer yet have actually recognized the contributions of cocurricular programs and included them in the enrollment management process.

For those cocurricular professionals who actively participate in enrollment management, it is another step in the evolutionary process of being recognized as an integral component in the educational system.

Frederick (1959) referred to the "suppression stage" when those controlling higher education viewed out-of-class involvements as frivolous and threatening. It was not very long before administrative leaders recognized that these activities had gained "immense popularity and significantly influenced students," and "sought to gain control over them (Miller, Winston & Mendenhall, 1983)." During this period the term extracurricular was common and tended to connote roles that were viewed as support or ancillary. Next came the long-sought status of being recognized as a partner with academic or curricular programs. This occurred when it was realized that student services, instead of merely offering programs, had progressed to "intentionally facilitating holistic development of students as an integral part of their formal education (Miller, Winston & Mendenhall, 1983)."

If this evolution is to continue, it certainly should include a partnership in enrollment management. For those institutions that feel a need to better control their enrollment and that embrace the Hossler model, looking for assistance from cocurricular areas is a natural step. Having long been recognized as major contributors to the quality of student life, cocurricular programs will most often be viewed by enrollment managers as retention agents. It should be noted that there exists many implications for recruitment and alumni relations as well.

Retention

It is the issue of quality of life and involvement in the institution that is critical to the retention of students. Out-of-class experiences enable students to view themselves as members of a community that offers more than an academic regimen. It is a balance of academic success and meaningful involvement in programs, activities, and organizations that creates student satisfaction which translates to retention.

Cocurricular experiences are as diverse as the student population which utilizes them. For one student, cocurricular involvement may be attending an on-campus movie, for another a noncredit aerobics class, for yet another a part-time job, participation in several intramural events, attendance at cultural programs, and membership (including leadership roles) in several student organizations. Regardless of the level of involvement, each student has made participation a priority and views these activities as important aspects of campus life.

Astin (1977) showed that cocurricular involvement is positively associated with persistence in school. Further, a thesis study by Dorelski and referenced by Power-Ross (1980) showed that involvement was the only significant variable applicable to student retention. These and other studies indicate that cocurricular experiences lead students to feel greater ties to the university and for those students involved in decision-making bodies such as founding boards or student government, a greater degree of ownership in the university. Participation in organizations contributes to student development by allowing for increased levels of self-confidence and self-esteem while developing lifelong communication, management, and leadership skills. Organizational membership also offers opportunities to interact with faculty and administrative advisors. These out-of-class contacts provide mentoring relationships as well as increased feelings of bonding with the institution.

Student organizations offer a wide range of experiences and fall into a variety of categories: all university governance or programming, performing arts, international, minority, departmental, honorary and professional, communication, fraternal, sports and leisure, service, and religious. Participation enables the student to establish friendships, experiment with career interests, expand upon academic programs, share in institutional decision making, and participate in special interest activities.

Other student activity programs are offered to satisfy the social, entertainment, recreational, and cultural tastes of the student population. An imaginative schedule of movies, dances, lectures, entertainers, and special events will contribute greatly to student satisfaction. The same will result from a well-organized and diverse offering of recreational programs.

The entire package of cocurricular programs, including student organizations, campus recreation, minority and international student services, social and cultural events all taking place in first-rate facilities, will serve students' physical, emotional, social, intellectual, and spiritual needs. As all of this occurs, student persistence is enhanced.

Retention of Special Populations
As retention is defined as one of the goals of enrollment management systems and as cocurricular programs are established as valuable retention agents, it is logical to examine the ramifications of these programs on students at particular retention risk. Segments of the student population, to include minority, international, nontraditional and even traditional, off-campus students, must make the same adjustments as all students, but also encounter other problems which make attrition more likely. While all cocurricular programs have tendencies to increase retention and should target all students, reality dictates that many such programs will fail to meet the needs of certain students. Special efforts designed to retain students transcend the need to keep total enrollment at desired levels. Institutional goals that include diversification of student population and internationalization make attempts to recruit and retain special populations imperative. Cocurricular programming must play a critical role in the institution's commitment to these students.

Much evidence exists which supports the notion that minorities at predominantly white institutions struggle to adjust to college life; a struggle not faced by their white counterparts. Mallenkrodt and Sedlacek (1987) spoke to this reality, "the time that successful black students must spend in developing a sense of community and an identification with the campus tends to be greater than that spent by white students." Ponce (1988) correlated "additional obstacles" to higher minority student attrition, and he and others use the terms isolation, rejection, and alienation to describe feelings experienced by minority students. As suggested by many, an institution-wide effort is needed to combat these obstacles to minority student success, and cocurricular programs have a long history of fostering a sense of belonging. The task is one of combining the efforts of student services areas which are designed primarily for minority students with those not so designated, to establish in the minds of minority students a feeling of ownership in both.

Much has been debated about the relevancy and effectiveness of minority student service programs and facilities but as Stennis-Williams, Terrell and Haynes (1988) wrote, "Not since the turbulent 1960s has there been such a groundswell of minority support for a place of their own on predominantly white campuses . . ." Opponents of this philosophy cite the need to "mainstream" minority students, and argue that minority student service programs and especially minority cultural centers exacerbate separation and perpetuate the barriers to a successful campus life. However, 71 percent of students in a 1987 Ohio State University stated that they felt a "need for special social, educational, and cultural programming." These students suggest that "programming of this nature is important to their adjustment to the university and that these programs might be enhanced if a special facility were designated for their use."

At the same time, however, every effort must be made to remove all obstacles, real and perceived, to minority student involvement in other organizations and programs. Student affairs professionals and especially cocurricular staff can make the inclusion of minority students into programs and organizations a more likely occurrence. There are many ways to facilitate this participation, including

- Assess the cocurricular needs of minority students
- Encourage minority students to participate in student government
- Conduct minority leadership development programs
- Help to promote and facilitate programs and events sponsored by minority organizations

- Encourage cosponsoring of events by minority/majority organizations
- Include minority students in the campus programming and funding boards; this is critical as it will not only help ensure programs of wider appeal but also help to assure minorities that they share in determining the direction of campus activities
- Use minority students as program and facility employees; having minorities in visible and responsible part-time jobs within program offices as well as supervisory positions in student unions and recreation facilities will create a positive image.

If these and other efforts are consistently and sincerely made and are in conjunction with a minority student services program that is properly housed, staffed, and funded, the quality of life for minority students will be reflected by their persistence.

Similar concerns exist for the acclimation of international students to the campus environment. These students often experience the isolation, alienation, and discrimination that has been related to the minority student experience. In some ways, it may be more difficult for international students. Their cultural experience is nearly always dramatically different from that of an American college campus; there are varying degrees of language barriers, different religious beliefs, and special dietary needs that make adjustment very difficult. While cocurricular programs cannot solve all these problems, they can produce opportunities for international students that will provide a more positive experience.

As with minority students, there is a need for international students to have programs that are designed to meet their unique needs. Professional staff, adequate programmatic funds, and an international student facility are the fundamentals of an international student services area which can begin to respond to the concerns of this student population.

As with minority student services, some will argue that these programs will further the separation and isolation of international students. International students, like minority students, are ardently supportive of the programs targeted for them, and without them the persistence of international students would be severely threatened.

In addition to staff, facilities, and operating budgets, the office of international student services might also strive to

- Provide a well-organized host family program matching an international student with a community family, especially during early stages of adjustment
- Develop and advise international student organizations
- Encourage international students to participate in other activities and organizations
- Provide and promote recreational programs that have particular appeal to international students, i.e., soccer, volleyball, table tennis, and badminton
- Provide adequate open hours during academic break periods for facilities used by international students; they are less likely to leave campus for break and have greater amounts of free time.

Special efforts also need to be made for off-campus students. This category includes nontraditional, commuter, and transfer students; each group possessing its own unique needs. While their plight does not seem as difficult as minority and international students, these students also battle against isolation although for them it may seem more like anonymity. Living on campus is always included in the list of factors which positively affect retention. Off-campus living, particularly for commuters, lends itself to a feeling of disenfranchisement. Without addressing problems like class availability or lack of parking for commuters, cocurricular staff can make a difference by

- Providing day-care services
- Making sure facilities are available and comfortable for those not living near campus, i.e., lounge and study areas, food service, recreation facilities
- Creating communication networks to get information about campus activities and events to these students
- Supporting off-campus and nontraditional organizations.

Recruitment

If, as has been argued, the cocurricular arm of an institution is a significant retention agent, what are the ramifications of this for the enrollment manager and what implications does this have for recruitment? It is doubtful that there is much that enrollment managers can or should do to shape the day-to-day course of cocurricular programs. These programs have existed and exerted their influence on retention long before the concept of enrollment management, as it is defined today, was introduced. Enrollment managers can, however, incorporate what they know to be the positive influences of quality cocurricular programs into the marketing of the institution.

There is, with any prospective student and his/her parents, a list of factors which influence the selection of a university. Somewhere in each individual's or family's list exists a category which includes cocurricular programs. While it may be prioritized beneath such items as academic reputation, availability of desired major or cost, it is often cited as an important factor.

In short, students and their parents are perceptive enough to want to know what opportunities exist for involvement outside of the classroom. The enrollment management team must be prepared to provide this information. The presentation of this information may mention retention statistics, discuss student development theory or give highlights of a lengthy menu of student activity options. It may be described in discussions, depicted in brochures, viewed on videos or highlighted on campus tours. Regardless of how the picture is painted, it will be more vivid if cocurricular practitioners are involved in the process. This can happen in a variety of ways:

- Top enrollment management staff should meet regularly with cocurricular staff to maintain knowledge of these programs
- The cocurricular background of potential admissions counselors should be considered in the hiring process
- Extensive sessions with cocurricular staff should be part of the training program for admission counselors
- Cocurricular staff members should participate in the

recruiting process whenever possible
- Students selected to support the recruiting process should have extensive cocurricular background
- Cocurricular facilities should be showcased in brochures and during campus tours
- Minority and international student services staff can be particularly helpful in recruitment by participating in campus visit programs and assisting in the preparation of written promotional materials for minority and international students
- Student activities and recreational sports can assist by planning events and activities to coincide with special campus visit programs
- Cocurricular staff can conduct on-campus programs for high school students designed, in part, to create interest in the institution (examples are leadership development or summer residential programs in conjunction with academic areas).

This is certainly not an exhaustive list of ways in which cocurricular programs and staff can aid in the recruiting process, but is designed to illustrate potential. Most of what is included is methods of communicating to prospective students the retention qualities of cocurricular programs.

Housing and Residential Life

Through both environmental control and program activity, an office or center for residential life is involved in the life of the whole student. Not only does it encompass the physical, social, and ethical concerns of the student, but it must create and manage an environment conducive to student development, both academic and personal. These goals are accomplished by performing specialized activities that relate directly to the university's enrollment management goals and by providing a support staff that is at once conscientious toward its duties and sensitive to the needs of the academic community by providing facilities sufficient to the academic, scholarly, cultural, and social needs of the individual student and the university community.

Specific goals of a center for housing and residential life as part of a university-wide enrollment management plan are:

- To maintain a physical environment which offers a safe, secure, and attractive place for students to live
- To provide a residential environment conducive to academic achievement
- To promote opportunities to engage in cultural and leisure time activities
- To encourage participation in social affairs contributing to social education
- To develop a group adequacy and individual personal satisfaction
- To evoke a philosophical habit through the practice of human understanding
- To develop further understanding of democracy growing from the opportunity to practice the precepts of cooperative democratic living
- To protect the rights of the university and the individual student.

Retention and the Residence Halls

A major factor in student retention is the presence of a productive residential life since this is the student's home away from home. If students are not satisfied with their living environment, they are less likely to be satisfied with the university in general. This, in turn, affects retention and ultimately recruitment. The housing and residential life offices stress the proactive approach rather than the reactive approach. The RA not only stands for resident advisor, but also for retention agent.

At a recent orientation meeting for new residence hall staff at Bradley University, several current resident advisors were asked to share with the group a rewarding experience that they had during their career on residence hall staff. Significantly, each of them described situations in which they had been instrumental in persuading frustrated students to continue their college education.

Since the resident advisor on the residence hall floor often becomes a "significant other," RAs are encouraged to quickly establish rapport with their residents by having individual meetings with them early in the semester and to then be not only available to their residents, but to also be approachable. In this way, opportunities for significant interaction between staff and residents are more likely to occur.

The staff person can be the front line to notice when a student is getting into trouble socially, emotionally, or academically. Resident advisors receive continuing training in peer counseling techniques, suicide prevention, crisis management, and conflict mediation, as well as training in how to refer students to resources available both on campus and in the community.

Management Style

The center for housing and residential life's management style, consistent with an enrollment management plan, is more participative than authoritarian and involves the students in the decision-making process with the guidance and supervision of the center. Emphasizing this management approach, residence hall directors and assistant hall directors are usually promoted from within after first serving as an assistant resident advisor and resident advisor, thus giving them at least two years of experience. These positions provide many undergraduate students with significant and invaluable leadership and management experience.

Students require a wide range of housing choices to fit almost any need. These housing choices include: coed freshman residence halls, upperclassman halls, freshman and upperclassman combined halls, coed floors, buildings that have all single rooms, fraternities, sororities, and a student apartment complex. Residence halls should be constructed to allow students to develop an identity by getting to know each other and to feel a sense of community.

One of the programs which several residence halls use to help develop community is that of student-directed communities.

All floors in the residence halls are encouraged to establish floor identities by choosing a floor name, electing officers, collecting a floor activity fund, and forming intramural sports teams. With the student-directed communities, residents go through a process of drafting a community charter which provides a structure for residents to be involved within their community. It also provides a forum for discussion of the individual and group rights and responsibilities.

The process of the student-directed communities and the developing of the floor charter encourage residents to take more responsibility for their behavior and hold one another more accountable by defining a mutual set of expectations. The basic expectations of resident hall members, discussed elsewhere in this chapter with the Statement of Fraternal Values and Ethics, becomes a part of the discussion process.

Students are also encouraged to participate in the leadership of their particular residence halls outside their immediate floor communities by becoming involved in their residence hall council. Each hall has a governing body which consists of representatives from each floor and an executive council. The council is responsible for planning hall activities and for suggesting changes in university residence hall policies. The council also handles resident suggestions for hall improvements.

Throughout the various programs, emphasis is on personal responsibility which is choice-based, placing the responsibility on the individual. Proactive decision making is stressed over the reactive approach, making decisions that place the individual students in control of themselves and their environment rather than responding to situations that are out of control. Students are encouraged to take responsibility for their own behavior.

The student-directed communities, the basic expectations, and intensive workshops with residence hall staff on ethics help to support this philosophy.

Opportunities for students to further enhance their leadership skills occur through organizing, planning, and participating in social, recreational, and educational activities. These include the training of residence hall staff and Greek officers to act as peer facilitators in leading programs on such topics as date rape, suicide prevention, communications, alcohol, and relationships.

Much emphasis is placed on training for the residence hall staff. In addition to previously mentioned programs, this training includes weekly meetings in individual residence halls; monthly in-service training and weeklong workshops at the beginning of each semester which include emergency procedures, student discipline, role playing and confrontation, individual counseling and communication skills, management techniques, programming implementation, drug and alcohol education, group decision making, suicide prevention, stress management, study skills and time management, cultural awareness, and campus and community resources.

Fraternities and Sororities

All residential campuses have some form of residence hall system and on many campuses, a major component of the housing and residential life system are the social fraternities and sororities commonly known as the Greek system.

In spite of the criticism of these organizations—elitism, anti-intellectual, hazing—in the past 10 years the Greek system on many campuses has expanded and grown at a phenomenal rate. If not properly managed, these organizations can be an embarrassment and legal liability to their parent institution. However, if they are properly supervised and guided they can be a major positive influence providing numerous leadership opportunities and they can have a significantly positive effect upon the institution's retention rate.

Basic Expectations

To lessen the disparity between fraternity ideals and individual behavior and to personalize these ideals in the daily undergraduate experience, the following basic expectations of fraternity membership have been established:

I. I will know and understand the ideals expressed in my fraternity ritual and will strive to incorporate them in my daily life.

II. I will strive for academic achievement and practice academic integrity.

III. I will respect the dignity of all persons; therefore, I will not physically, mentally, psychologically, or sexually abuse or haze any human being.

IV. I will protect the health and safety of all human beings.

V. I will respect my property and the property of others; therefore, I will neither abuse nor tolerate the abuse of property.

VI. I will meet my financial obligations in a timely manner.

VII. I will neither use nor support the use of illegal drugs; I will neither abuse nor support the abuse of alcohol.

VIII. I acknowledge that a clean and attractive environment is essential to both physical and mental health; therefore, I will do all in my power to see that the chapter property is properly cleaned and maintained.

Because the Greek system represents in its purest form, the student-directed community, a significant amount of outside supervision is necessary. This supervision takes the form of faculty advisors, alumni advisors, and generally a university administrator who coordinates the Greek system.

The organizational capacity and vitality of these groups can be overwhelming. Weekly and sometimes daily monitoring of their activities is crucial.

Because of the high turnover of membership and leadership of these organizations, workshops for the major officers must be presented each semester.

On most campuses, the Greek population is a distinct minority. However, they are highly visible. Because of their living accommodations and their social structure, they must be very carefully monitored so that they are not at odds with the mission of the university.

Summary

The first part of this chapter discussed the role of an institution's cocurricular programs in the enrollment management process. It was argued that true enrollment management systems are highly integrated and need to seek contributions from all components of the institution.

Cocurricular programs have as their primary objective the facilitation of a high quality of life and student development through the provision of programs, organizations, facilities, and activities. The immediate benefit to enrollment management is a significant contribution to student persistence. The values of cocurricular programs can also be incorporated into the recruitment process and cocurricular staff can play an important role in this effort. The likelihood of successful outcomes awaiting the student following graduation is also enhanced by involvement in cocurricular programs.

To conclude, if an institution is seeking to optimize its enrollment and settles upon an enrollment management strategy, it would do well to enlist the assistance of its cocurricular programs and staff.

References

Astin, A.W. (1977). *Four critical years: Effects of college on beliefs, attitudes and knowledge.* San Francisco: Jossey-Bass Publisher.

Frederick, R.W. (1959). *The third curriculum.* New York: Appleton, Century and Crofts.

Hossler, D. (1984). *Enrollment management: An integrated approach.* New York: College Entrance Examination Board.

Hossler, D. (1986). *Creating effective enrollment management systems.* New York: College Entrance Examination Board.

Mallenkrodt, B., and Sedlacek, W.E. (1987). Student retention and the use of facilities by race. *NASPA Journal,* 24(3), 28–32.

Miller, T.K.; Winston, R.B.; and Mendenhall, W.R. (1983). *Human development and higher education administration and leadership in student affairs.* Muncie, Indiana: Accelerated Development, Inc.

Ponce, F.Q. (1988). Minority student retention: A moral and legal imperative. In M.C. Terrell and D.J. Wright (eds.),

From Survival to Success: Promoting Minority Student Retention (pp. 1–17). Washington, D.C.: National Association of Student Personnel Administrators.

Power-Ross, S.J. (1980). Cocurricular activities validated through research. *Student Activities Programming,* 13(6), 46–48.

Stennis-Williams, S.; Terrell, M.C.; and Haynes, A.W. (1988). The emergent role of multicultural education centers on predominantly white campuses. In M.C. Terrell and D.J. Wright (eds.), *From Survival to Success: Promoting Minority Student Retention* (pp. 73–96). Washington, D.C.: National Association of Student Personnel Administrators.

Chapter 9

Student Affairs, Enrollment Management, and the University

Alan Galsky

In higher education as in other professions words and terms and/or concepts appear that did not formerly exist. These terms or concepts are initiated to describe a new process that formerly did not exist or existed in fragmented parts. This new process is usually implemented to deal with a new, critical problem. As a result this new term or process becomes extremely popular, an *in* thing, an often-cited term—in short, a "hot item."

One such new term in the jargon of higher education is enrollment management. This concept stems from a variety of factors, including the demographic data which predicted a shrinking pool of high school graduates from 1979–96 (McConnell & Kaufman, 1984), the increased speculation among certain population groups of students about the value of a higher education (Arbecter, 1987; Estrada, 1988), the increasing costs of higher education, and the continued policy changes at the federal and state governments which have resulted in less direct aid to college students (O'Keefe, 1987).

These factors have affected all schools and, for many, have threatened their viability or survival. As a result the need to manage or control student enrollment has become important on many campuses and for some a necessity for survival.

What does this term enrollment management mean and, more important, how is it best implemented? There are many definitions for enrollment management (Hossler, 1984, 1986; Kemerer et al, 1982). The keys to any definition, however, are that enrollment management is more than a term, it is a philosophy and a strategy, one that must be implemented and believed on a university-wide basis if it is to be meaningful and have the best chance for success.

Comprehensive enrollment management must ask the following questions:

1. What types of students (quality and quantity) does this institution want (or must) have?
2. What strategies and plans are necessary to have the best chance of recruiting these students to the university?
3. What services, activities, and programs must the university have in place to ensure these students receive a quality educational experience and thus enhance the chances that these students will remain at the university and graduate? (There is probably no better spokesperson for the university than a satisfied student!)
4. What programs and services must the university provide these students to help them upon graduation with job placement, or professional or graduate school placement?

Whatever the answers to these questions, the plans cannot be implemented by one office or one individual. Instead, enrollment management must be a university-wide commitment, supported by the administration but administered by many offices and individuals at the university.

Enrollment Management
and Student Affairs

A successful enrollment management plan must involve a comprehensive division of student affairs since the division is responsible for recruiting, housing, developing, testing, orienting, advising, entertaining, disciplining, and placing the students. In short, the division makes the first contact with the student (and the parents), provides constant contact through a myriad of activities and programs during the student's time at the university, and plays a pivotal role in helping to place that student when the student graduates from the university, to best utilize the student's talents. The division of student affairs must be at the heart of the enrollment management plan, the cheerleader for implementing a university-wide commitment to enrollment management and must serve as a role model for the rest of the university in their commitment and dedication to successfully implementing a comprehensive enrollment management plan.

The Enrollment Management Committee
With any successful plan, some individual(s) must be responsible for developing and implementing the plan, overseeing the plan, revising and nurturing the plan. In short, even with total university support for an enrollment management plan integrated within a division of student affairs or closely associated with a division of student affairs as described by Zucker in Chapter Three, someone must have direct responsibility for the plan. While everyone should be involved in enrollment management, there has to be administrative enrollment managers.

Along with the concept and strategy of enrollment management there has evolved the position of enrollment manager. These individuals should be energetic, enthusiastic, and extremely knowledgeable of admissions, financial assistance, marketing concepts, and computer technology. They are well paid and in high demand. A successful university enrollment management plan and operation must have a highly talented professional individual in the position of enrollment manager. The exact title is less important than the individual's talents, dedication, and commitment to enrollment management at the university.

The conception, development, and implementation of an enrollment management plan for the university is too important, too complex, and involves too many facets of the university to be the responsibility of any single individual (enrollment manager) no matter how talented.

The responsibility for this critical function should rest with a committee: the enrollment management committee. The exact composition of this committee is not cast in stone, but should consist of individuals knowledgeable in enrollment management and have talents that complement one another. These individuals should be well known and well respected by the university community. The composition of the enrollment management committee may consist of the following:

- The chief student affairs officer: This is extremely important if the division of student affairs is going to take a leadership role in implementing institution-wide enrollment management strategies. In addition, the chief student affairs officer has contact with a wide range of university administrators which makes it easier to implement a university-wide comprehensive enrollment management plan.
- The executive director of enrollment management or chief enrollment manager officer: This individual must be able to help shape the plan, determine its feasibility for the institution, and be responsible for implementing the heart of the plan and for monitoring the plan. This individual must have overall responsibility for admissions and financial assistance.
- An associate director for enrollment management: This individual could have specific operational responsibilities for transfer enrollment, minority recruitment, international student recruitment, and the operating budget for enrollment management.
- An associate director for enrollment management: This individual could have direct responsibility for financial assistance, university scholarships, and publications.

[handwritten marginalia: 2 associates ? ?]

The main function of the enrollment management committee is to develop, implement, revise when necessary, and monitor the enrollment management plan. It must be clear to all at the university that decisions regarding enrollment management operation and strategy are made by the enrollment management committee. The committee must have this authority if the enrollment management plan is going to be successful. The committee also has the authority and freedom to interact with, when necessary, key members of the university's administration.

Typical questions discussed by the enrollment management committee include:

1. Are the objectives of the enrollment management plan consistent with the institution's academic mission and goals?
2. Is the admissions and financial assistance staff adequate to carry out the recruitment objectives of the enrollment management plan?
3. What new geographic markets should be explored?
4. Is the financial assistance budget adequate to successfully carry out the enrollment management plan?
5. How many freshman and transfer students is it possible or desirable to recruit in the fiscal year?
6. Are the enrollment management publications adequate to complement the enrollment management plan?
7. What is the total budget (admissions, financial assistance, publication) necessary to successfully implement the enrollment management plan for that year?
8. Is the computer technology serving the enrollment management operation sufficient?

The enrollment management committee usually meets on a weekly basis for two-three hours and has a set agenda. The "give and take" at these meetings, the ability to challenge statements by other members, the ability to critically and objectively review the enrollment management plan and fine-tune adjustments or make revisions is critical to the success of the overall plan. The committee members may not always agree with one another, but they should respect one another. The meetings are not always smooth, but they are stimulating. The results of these weekly sessions and at least two to three all-day retreats throughout the year is a carefully developed and successfully implemented comprehensive, institution-wide

enrollment management plan. A typical agenda for an enrollment management committee is presented in Figure 1.

Figure 1
ENROLLMENT MANAGEMENT
COMMITTEE AGENDA

1. Analysis of freshman enrollment for fall
2. Analysis of out-of-state enrollment for fall
3. Analysis of transfer and minority enrollment for fall
4. Plans to enroll desired freshman and transfer class for fall
5. Residence halls of the future
6. Student telephone programs
7. Student search
8. Plans for counselors' luncheon and breakfast
9. Plans for summer receptions and interviews
10. Update on enrollment in specific targeted areas
11. Plans to obtain the services of a special recruiter for the music
    program for fall
12. Update on east coast admissions position
13. Current situation on admission budget
14. Publications
15. Merit scholarships
16. Preliminary financial assistance form summary
17. Update on initial financial assistance awards
18. Plans for enrollment management summer retreat
19. Other business

The Relationship of the Committee
to the Division of Student Affairs
and the University

If the division of student affairs is to take the leadership role in
adopting and employing institution-wide enrollment management strategies then enrollment management must be the
responsibility of a comprehensive division of student affairs.
The director of enrollment management and the associate
directors must report directly to the chief student affairs officer
or, as is discussed in Chapter Three, must interact with the chief
student affairs officer.

The executive director of enrollment management and the
two associate directors are members of the executive directors'

committee of the division of student affairs. This committee has the responsibility for implementing student affairs policy for the university, and each of the directors and associate directors for enrollment management present reports at the weekly executive directors' meetings. The other members of the executive directors' committee are in charge of key offices and administer programs and activities that are essential to a successful institution-wide enrollment management plan. All of the executive directors work closely with one another to implement the university-wide plan. Each of the executive directors' programs and activities are discussed and reviewed as to how these programs and activities will help implement the university-wide plan.

Rationale for Investing University Resources In Enrollment Management

The shrinking pool of high school graduates, the increase in minority and nontraditional students and the changing support of government for higher education over the next 10 years will make the successful recruitment of students and the management of enrollment critical. For some schools a successful enrollment management plan will help fine-tune an already healthy situation; for some schools this plan will help change strategies and/or directions in enrollment and for others it will mean survival. A successful plan, however, for any school will require resources for personnel, scholarships, and financial assistance and for the myriad of programs and activities that must be carried out in order to have a successful enrollment management plan.

It is up to the enrollment management committee to ensure that the proper resources are committed by the university to support the plan. This may not be easy, especially if resources are limited and there are many demands for those resources. It is, therefore, necessary that the enrollment management committee present a well-conceived plan to the administration and emphasize the importance of funding this plan. It should defend its plan forcefully and persuasively.

However, no university can afford to be without a sound enrollment management plan and thus must find and commit the resources for this plan. It is a small price to pay to manage an enrollment successfully. For some who support the successful plan it will mean survival; for others, it will mean the luxury of being able to enroll a freshman class that is optimum for the university.

Cooperation of Other Areas in Successfully Implementing an Enrollment Strategy

An enrollment management plan that incorporates the major role and responsibility for the division of student affairs is the first step, although very critical, toward successful implementation of a university-wide enrollment management plan. For this plan to be successful, it must have the involvement and support of the university community from the board of trustees to the students.

Involving the President and the Board
The president and the board of trustees must fully support the university's commitment to enrollment management. This support must be clearly articulated to the rest of the university. It is the responsibility of the enrollment management committee in general and the chief student affairs officer specifically to ensure the president and the board of trustees are committed both verbally and financially to a university-wide enrollment management plan.

If the chief student affairs officer meets with the trustees on a regular basis, which is the case at many universities, he/she should update the board on the progress of the enrollment management plan and constantly reinforce to the trustees how this plan must involve a university-wide commitment. The chief student affairs officer in his/her meeting with the president should continue to update the president on the progress of the plan and the university's support of the plan. It is up to the chief student affairs officer and the enrollment management committee to educate the board and president on the concepts of enrollment management.

Involving the Vice Presidents

If a university-wide enrollment plan is going to be supported by the administration, it must also receive the support of the vice presidents for business affairs and development. Each of these individuals must in their own organizations show support for and emphasize a university-wide enrollment philosophy. The vice president for business affairs' support for the financial commitment to an enrollment management plan is critical; the support of the vice president to the individuals who cash students' checks to the maintenance workers is also important. There can be no loose links in the chain if the university-wide concept is going to be successful.

The vice president for development must also be committed to the plan. The vice president's support is critical in the areas of fund raising and alumni and parent relations.

Involving Academic Deans and Faculty

The successful implementation of a university-wide enrollment plan must have the support of the academic deans. These individuals must be the cheerleaders for this plan among the department chairs and the faculty. There is constant demand on the deans, chairs, and faculty in a university-wide plan to meet with prospective students and parents, speak to groups of students and parents on special visit days, play a key role in summer orientation programs, and call prospective students. Without the prior commitment of the deans and faculty to this plan, it will be difficult to continue to ask and receive their assistance. Students and parents want to meet with faculty and should be able to do so!

The best way to ensure the commitment of the academic deans to a university-wide enrollment management plan is for the student affairs and academic areas of the university to have an excellent, collegial relationship. One way to foster such a relationship is to have the chief student affairs officer report to the academic provost and meet with the academic council of deans. Although this structure in which the student affairs division reports to the academic provost occurs only 15 percent of the time (Robinson & Boatwright, 1987), it is a very work-able model, a model which ensures an excellent relationship between the academic and student affairs division, a model which helps ensure the successful implementation of a university-wide enrollment management plan and results in providing the atmosphere and environment that many of the leading educators have found missing or lacking in the undergraduate experience (Boyer, 1987).

At the regular meetings of the council of deans all enrollment management plans involving academic faculty and deans are thoroughly discussed and agreement is reached before the specific plan is implemented. While there is not always harmonious agreement on these plans, there is always a frank, stimulating exchange of views on these concepts. It is essential at these meetings that the chief student affairs officer or spokesperson for enrollment management be willing to compromise when necessary, but not yield to the pressure of the academic deans on important issues.

Involving Students
It is important in the successful implementation of a university-wide enrollment management plan to have the support of the student body. In many cases one of the factors involved in the decision to attend a university is the general reactions to the student body or individual students during a campus visit.

The best way to ensure the students' support of a university-wide enrollment management plan is for the chief student affairs officer to inform the student leaders about the enrollment management plan, the importance of the plan, and their role in the successful implementation of the plan. The chief student affairs officer should have many opportunities during his/her meetings with the student leaders (e.g., student senate, student advisory committee) to educate, inform, and involve students in the university-wide plan.

University Politics and Enrollment Management

Perhaps the biggest stumbling block to the successful implementation of a university-wide enrollment plan may be internal university politics. Arguments over money, philosophy, continuation of various programs, and related matters could initially curtail or hinder the successful implementation of a university-wide plan.

The success of this plan for most institutions is too important and too urgent to allow politics to interfere, but that does not preclude such interference. The only way to work through most of these politics is to involve all aspects of the university community, most importantly the key players, in this plan and indicate to them that their involvement and support is critical. This will take some time, but the time is well spent.

In the end, however, the enrollment management committee must be willing to take some risks, to put their position and credibility on the line, if necessary, to push their plan through the grasp of university politics.

This, at times, will not be easy, but stakes are high and the plan is critical, and no one said it is going to be easy. If an institution wants a plan, some entity must be responsible for its implementation, regardless of the roadblocks!

- The execu   nagement or
  chief enroll   idual must be
  able to help   sibility for the
  institution,   ting the heart
  of the plan   his individual
  must have   sions and fi-
  nancial assi

References

Arbecter, S. (1987). Black enrollment. *Change,* 19, 14–19.

Boyer, E.L. (1987) *College—The undergraduate experience in America.* New York: Harper and Row.

Estrada, L.F. (1988). Anticipating the demographic future: Dramatic changes are on the way, *Change* 20, 14–19.

Hossler, D. (1984). *Enrollment management: An integrated approach.* New York: The College Board.

Hossler, D. (1986). *Creating effective enrollment management systems.* New York: The College Board.

Kemerer, F.; Baldridge, J.V.; and Green, K. (1982). *Strategies for effective enrollment management.* Washington, D.C.: American Association of State Colleges and Universities.

McConnell, W.R., and Kaufman, N. (1984). *High school graduates: Projection for the fifty states (1982–2000).* Boulder, CO: Western Interstate Commission for Higher Education.

O'Keefe, M. (1987). A new look at college costs: Where does the money really go. *Change* 19, 2–34.

Robinson, D.C., and Boatwright, M.A. (1987). *National association of student personnel administrators salary survey 1987–88.* Washington, D.C.: National Association of Student Personnel Administration, Inc.

NASPA Publications
ORDER FORM

	Quantity	Cost
The Invisible Leaders: Student Affairs Mid-manager $7.95 members, $9.95 nonmembers	_____	_____
The New Professional: A Resource Guide for New Student Affairs Professionals and Their Supervisors. $7.95 members, $9.95 nonmembers	_____	_____
From Survival to Success: Promoting Minority Student Retention. $7.95 members, $9.95 nonmembers	_____	_____
Student Affairs and Campus Dissent. $5.95 members, $7.50 nonmembers	_____	_____
Alcohol Policies and Procedures on College and University Campuses $5.95 members, $7.50 nonmembers	_____	_____
Opportunities for Student Development in Two-Year Colleges. $5.95 members, $7.50 nonmembers	_____	_____
Private Dreams, Shared Visions: Student Affairs Work in Small Colleges. $5.95 members, $7.50 nonmembers	_____	_____

	Quantity	Cost
Promoting Values Development in College Students. $5.95 members, $7.50 nonmembers	_____	_____
Translating Theory into Practice: Implications of Japanese Management Theory for Student Personnel Administrators. $5.95 members, $7.50 nonmembers	_____	_____
Risk Management and the Student Affairs Professional. $5.95 members, $7.50 nonmembers	_____	_____
Career Perspectives in Student Affairs. $5.95 members, $7.50 nonmembers	_____	_____
Points of View. $5 members, $7 nonmembers	_____	_____
Issues and Perspectives on Academic Integrity. $1 members, $1.50 nonmembers	_____	_____
NASPA Journal, $35 annual subscription, $9.50 single copy. If single issue, indicate volume and issue:_____	_____	_____
TOTAL	_____	_____

Please return completed form with check, money order, or credit card authorization. Return to: NASPA, 1700 18th Street, NW, Suite 301, Washington, D.C. 20009-2508; (202) 265-7500.

Payment enclosed ☐   Bill my credit card ☐

VISA ☐   MasterCard ☐   Expiration Date _____

Account Number _____ Signature _____

Please print

Name _____ NASPA Membership ID No. _____

Institution _____

Address _____

City _____ State _____ Zip _____